# Government Proposals
## CUTTING THROUGH THE CHAOS

# Government Proposals
## CUTTING THROUGH THE CHAOS

*Rebecca L. Shannon*

ffff
**MANAGEMENT**CONCEPTS
Vienna, Virginia

**((**
**MANAGEMENT**CONCEPTS

8230 Leesburg Pike, Suite 800
Vienna, Virginia 22182
Phone: (703) 790-9595
Fax: (703) 790-1371
Web: www.managementconcepts.com

Printed in the United States of America

**Library of Congress Cataloging-in-Publication Data**

Shannon, Rebecca L., 1951–
    Government proposals : cutting through the chaos / Rebecca L. Shannon.
      p. cm.
    Includes index.
    ISBN 1-56726-126-4 (hc.)
      1. Proposal writing in public contracting—United States. 2. Requests for
proposals (Public contracts)—United States. 3. Public contracts—United States.
4. Letting of contracts—United States. 5. Government purchasing—United
States. 6. Government purchasing—Law and legislation—United States. I. Title.

HD3861.U6 S5 2001
658.8'04—dc21

                                                                00-067887

To Hamid

# *About the Author*

Rebecca Shannon received a B.A. in English from Wilson College and an M.A. in English from New York University. She has 16 years of experience in proposals, first as an editor and production manager with Computer Technology Associates and later as a consulting writer and proposal manager. As a consultant, she has worked for AT&T, Hughes Information Technology Corporation, Booz, Allen & Hamilton, NCI Information Systems, and many other small and large companies in the Washington metropolitan region. She lives in Washington, D.C., where she fights hard to have a life outside the office.

# Table of Contents

# *Preface*

I've been around the proposal business for 16 years, first as a technical editor and later as a production manager and proposal development consultant—a fancy name for proposal writer that encompasses other things that the consultant does besides writing.

Along the way, I've been in and out of many companies, watching people as they perform in the role of proposal coordinator, also called proposal manager. Occasionally, I've held the position myself. During this time, I've met many disgruntled employees and frustrated consultants, many of whom don't understand—and some of whom don't want to understand—why things don't run more smoothly.

The situation would be as amusing as it is lucrative if I didn't know plenty of people in the various roles associated with proposal development who have real stress-related health problems. They suffer from asthma, gain and then lose 20 pounds in one month, have persistent indigestion from living on junk food, and suffer constant sleep deprivation. Others have only a smidgen of a life outside the office or live uneasily with little job satisfaction.

If you thrive on chaos or prefer denial, fine. I have met people who appear to live on the excitement of extreme deadlines. But not many of them. I want to be able to produce winning proposals in a stress-free environment so I can continue using the skills I've honed without dying before my time. I want other folks who find themselves managing a proposal process that has run amuck to be able to do the same.

With that objective in mind, I've taken a long look at the job, the companies in which I've worked, and the people who have managed proposals in those companies. I've found that the proposal coordinator's function is different from most corporate functions. The proposal coordinator draws from resources across the organization, such as telecommunications and computer support, security, marketing, and sales. He interacts in an ongoing way with senior-level managers throughout the organization. And he relies on people with whom he has no supervisory relationship to meet deadlines and produce products that will meet government requirements while working toward one immutable deadline after another.

Some of the characteristics of proposals and the proposal coordinator's position can't be changed: A government representative occasionally appears to take untoward glee in extending a deadline at the last minute; the requests for proposals (RFPs) for two important procurements end up on the same timeline; and your favorite consultant is gainfully engaged just when you need her.

But there are other aspects of the position that are not cast in stone and these can be changed or set up to work properly in the first place. To that end, I've analyzed methods, procedures, policies, and personal characteristics that contribute to or detract from the proposal process. I've asked, "Why is this process flowing so smoothly?" or "Why do I hate being here?"

In answering these questions, I've arrived at two basic models for running proposals. One I call the "support manager" model, in which the proposal coordinator focuses largely on the process of developing and producing proposals, paying little attention to the substance of the end product. The other model is the "value-added" model, in which the proposal coordinator shepherds the process while also tending to the form and content of the proposal.

Confusion about which model you're using and about who is responsible for what is the major source of stress in the proposal environment. Accordingly, I believe that it is imperative to take a hard look at the model at work in your organization.

I've also found that some methods, procedures, and policies have greater potential for producing a winning proposal in a stress-free environment than others. Explaining these methods, procedures, and policies—and inspiring you to use them—is the purpose of this guide.

This book speaks most directly to people who are in the position to establish a proposal process from scratch or to correct a dysfunctional process that is producing proposals but not winning business. These readers might be proposal coordinators or their managers, typically directors or vice presidents of business development or marketing.

So that you understand the context in which the proposal coordinator works, I lay some groundwork in Chapter 1, where I describe the basic procurement process and point you to two important documents: the Federal Acquisition Regulation (FAR) and the Freedom of Information Act

(FOIA). I also review the basic components of an RFP and the final product, the proposal, so you'll understand the terms used throughout the rest of the book.

In Chapter 2, I introduce the main players in developing and producing a proposal. Then I define my two basic models for producing proposals and the factors that influence how a model will work in a particular corporate environment with different personality types. This chapter covers the built-in challenges associated with the proposal coordinator's dual role and helps you assess the corporate and personal factors that work for or against you. It is meant to be an objective assessment for the purpose of clarification—not an exercise in assigning blame.

You'll forgive me for practicing some amateur psychology. I think that some examination of how various personalities function in the role of proposal coordinator is essential to setting the stage for a workable proposal process. Chapter 2 also offers suggestions for talking with your management about the proposal process and changing the attitudes and atmosphere surrounding proposals. If you're in a position to manage the proposal process from a high level—as a vice president of business development, for example—this chapter will also help you evaluate better the skills required in each of the proposal models, the type of process you want to implement, and the type of person who will best fill the role of proposal coordinator in your organization.

Chapter 3 explains what you'll need from your manager, if you're a proposal coordinator, or what the proposal coordinator needs from you, if you're a higher level manager. I need not reiterate the importance of knowing that your manager understands the advantages of a solid proposal process or the importance of the proposal coordinator in keeping that process in place so that the senior manager can stay out of the proposal business most of the time.

In Chapter 4, I show you how to create the support materials you will need to guide the design team in developing the proposal: to ensure the physical safety of the proposal and to set up the office for the comfort and convenience of the team. While you're doing that, you'll also be tracking RFPs on the Internet, as I describe in Chapter 5; sending out FOIA requests, if relevant; and participating in bid/no bid decisions.

Always, you will keep an eye toward production and plan for it accordingly, as I describe in Chapter 6. From the beginning of the proposal process to the end, you'll prepare for the final printed version of the proposal and the soft-copy submission, where necessary. This includes determining the size of exhibits in advance, creating soft-copy styles, and setting up templates for standard parts of the proposal (such as cover pages and tables of contents).

Before the design team arrives, you'll want to determine exactly what the team will need, clarify jobs, outline the proposal, and plan for proposal kickoff. These activities are the subject of Chapter 7. Chapter 8 finds you in the middle of the process, when the team will be storyboarding, writing, and piecing together the components of the proposal.

If you stay ahead of the game and coach your reviewers on providing constructive criticism, the review process, discussed in Chapter 9, should be a positive event that supports the proposal team and enhances the proposal. And if you have looked forward to the final production during every step of the process, the ultimate printed document, addressed in Chapter 10, will emerge with great fanfare but little frustration.

A few members of the proposal team and the proposed contract staff may be required to work past proposal submission to an oral presentation. Because oral presentations have become more popular in recent years, I address them in Chapter 11, offering you the benefit of my experience—and mistakes—in this area.

In Chapter 12, I look at the day-to-day activities of the proposal coordinator and wind the process down to its ultimate end, the debriefing or the win party.

The remainder of the book consists of practical checklists and examples. They apply to whatever model of proposal development you use and whatever manner of product or service you provide.

They also apply no matter what technologies you use now or what technological inventions follow in the next few years. I've tried to stay out of the discussion of technologies as much as possible, because even seemingly minor hardware and software choices today have enormous implications. Your choice of production hardware and software, while very important to the proposal process in its ability to affect the level of stress, has implications across the corporation. Even as I write this, I am wondering what format our boilerplate will take on our newly created corporate intranet.

Although the speed of technology is fast approaching the speed of light, very little that I write here—with the exception of the words on tracking RFPs—is dependent on a particular technology. As long as products and services are purchased on the basis of overall value rather than price alone, the government will ask for proposals and companies will write and produce them in some form. How you write and produce them is your choice. Neither advice nor support materials are helpful unless you put th′   ᵗo use. The underlying success or failure of a proposal process lies in the ⌣_ ⌣i-plined use of that process. If you don't use the materials and apply the process, reading this book will do you little good.

Finally, in an effort to avoid the personal pronoun conundrum, I use "he" and "she" interchangeably and arbitrarily. I also use the term "marketing" in its more general sense—as a one-word synonym for business development. In some organizations, the marketing department focuses only on analyzing competitors, developing and launching products, advertising, and the like. In other companies, the marketing department encompasses all business development activities, including developing and producing proposals. I'm thinking of the latter.

Enjoy and use.

*Rebecca L. Shannon*
*Washington, D.C.*
*December 2000*

# Acknowledgments

I wrote this book because people always say that you should write about what you know, and I know something about proposals. Proposals put food on my table and pay my mortgage. Proposals have also led me to meet some very good people who have participated in my professional and personal education and training, most importantly Barbara Lovelace of Winning Solutions, Inc., who gave me my first proposal-writing job, and Cathy Petrick, then of AT&T Federal Systems, who made that first job fun. Oh, what a time it was.

I received encouragement along the way from Jane Ashley Heavey, Kathy Sheridan, and Charlie Browne—my group—and space from Hamid Amiri, who can be an attention-grabber when he chooses. At work, most recently I get to test my theories on Bill Davis, Al Walke, Mike Rodgers, and Mark Crockett, who try very hard not to listen to a thing I say.

And always in the background is Brad Blanton, who reminds me that I truly can create my own life.

## CHAPTER 1

# *Setting the Context*

A successful process for responding to government solicitations begins with building a relationship with the prospective customer and ends with contract negotiations. Meanwhile, the two parties to the solicitation—the government and the offeror—perform numerous activities. Some companies that work on large acquisitions have developed process flows covering hundreds of activities associated with the solicitation process; the process for these companies can take months or even years.

The process I outline here is shorter, and the companies that I have in mind are smaller—they are mid-sized companies bidding mid-sized proposals. I'd be tempted to throw out a contract amount to define a mid-sized proposal or a baseline corporate revenue to define company size, but these fluctuate so wildly by industry that numbers end up being meaningless. A construction company might produce a relatively small proposal for a $150 million-dollar contract; a company specializing in facility management might produce the same size proposal for a $25 million-dollar contract; and a software support company might produce the equivalent proposal for a $10 million-dollar contract.

In my experience, however, the steps listed below are the major steps. As the procurement grows larger, substeps emerge. If the procurement is smaller, some steps are dropped altogether.

## THE SOLICITATION PROCESS

The keys steps in the solicitation process are:

1. *Researching the organization.* Marketing personnel cultivate relationships with agency contracting or technical staff, becoming familiar with the agency's mission and priorities. They try to uncover the customer's stated and unstated requirements so that they can be addressed specifically in subsequent proposals. At least, this is the ideal. On many occasions and in many types of companies, very little research is done before the RFP is on the street.

2. *Tracking the request for proposals.* Marketing personnel follow the development of a *request for proposals (RFP)*, the government's vehicle for acquiring services and products. They do this through direct contact with an agency or through a third-party vehicle, such as the *Commerce Business Daily*, known fondly as the CBD. The CBD is a daily listing of RFPs that are moving through the government's acquisition process.

In response to a CBD announcement or a later announcement through another medium, marketing personnel submit the company's name for inclusion on the *bid list*, a list of companies that will receive copies of the RFP and any communications regarding the solicitation. Bid lists show who your competitors or possible teammates for a solicitation might be.

Marketing personnel might also submit a Freedom of Information Act (FOIA) request for information on the current contract, if one exists. I will discuss RFPs more specifically later in this section, as well as the Freedom of Information Act. I will address the CBD more explicitly in Chapter 5.

3. *Issuing a draft RFP and request for comment.* The government issues a draft RFP with a request for comment, or RFC. In this step, the government gains information from potential contractors about the products and services that are currently on the market. Though the government is not required to be responsive to contractor comments, government RFP developers probably listen to large product manufacturers and service providers when these contractors comment about: (1) the capabilities currently on the market and those that will be on the market in the future, or (2) impractical or impossible requirements.

In some smaller procurements, this step is dropped altogether. When a draft is provided, you should take advantage of the opportunity to comment, as discussed in Chapter 5.

4. *Releasing the RFP.* The government releases an RFP outlining specifications for the products or services it wants to acquire and the proposal format. The standard RFP includes cover sheets, Sections A through M, and any number of attachments. The format of each section is tailored to suit the procuring organization and yet standardized to comply with the Federal Acquisition Regulation (FAR), a tome listing each and every itsy bitsy regulation ever conceived to irritate contractors or government personnel. The RFP also lists all FAR regulations

or formal standards that are considered pertinent to the acquisition and deemed to be part of the RFP by reference. More about this below.

5. *Holding a bid/no bid conference.* The offeror holds an informal or formal *bid/no bid meeting* to decide whether or not to bid on this job. The meeting could be a chat among managers or a structured, point-by-point analysis of the competition by an outside consultant. Studies by management organizations indicate that an accurate preliminary assessment of the competition and your chances of winning the solicitation increase the company's overall win percentage. By choosing not to bid on longshots, the company also saves money.

    In my experience, when smaller companies decide not to bid on a contract, they often fail to explore teaming opportunities with other companies (which are usually listed on the bid list). If your strategic plan involves getting work with a particular agency and you're not yet big enough to win your own contract with that agency, don't overlook teaming opportunities that will provide you with an "in." If you demonstrate your competence as a subcontractor, you will develop your performance credentials to win bigger contracts. You can read more about this in Chapter 5.

6. *Holding a pre-bid conference.* The government holds a *pre-bid conference* to provide additional information to contractors on the content of the RFP. During this formal presentation, the government may or may not answer on-the-spot questions. Sometimes the government accepts written questions at the pre-bid conference that are answered at a later date with other written questions, as described in the next bullet. I'll discuss attendance at pre-bid meetings and strategies associated with submitting questions to the government in Chapter 7.

7. *Responding to written questions.* Contractors submit written questions to the government, which compiles the questions, answers them in writing, and distributes the answers to all companies on the bid list.

8. *Developing and producing the proposal.* Contractors begin writing the proposal, carrying out the process that I describe in the rest of the book.

9. *Issuing amendments.* The government issues an amendment, another amendment, and another amendment, until you don't know what's in and what's out. I discuss how to log amendments in Chapter 12.

10. *Delivering the proposal.* Contractors submit their proposals at the appointed hour on the appointed day.

11. *Evaluating the proposal.* A team of reviewers called the source selection authority, which may consist of government personnel or government and contractor personnel, evaluates the proposal relative to specified standards. The proposal can be evaluated by all reviewers as a single entity, or it can be divided among reviewers who evaluate only a single element, such as the technical, management, or cost volume. The evaluation can be a single review that results in an award, or it can lead to one or all of the steps listed below.

12. *Issuing clarification requests and deficiency reports.* The government sometimes issues to each offeror an individualized list of clarifications and deficiencies, known as Cs and Ds or CRs and DRs. This usually occurs several months after the proposal has been submitted, when the reviewers have had an opportunity to look at and compare all the proposals that were submitted. The cycle of issuing and responding to Cs and Ds can repeat several times.

13. *Responding to clarification requests and deficiency reports.* The offeror responds to the Cs and Ds, often producing direct answers to the government's question as well as *change pages* to the proposal. Change pages are substitutions of new pages for old, and they can be a production pain in the neck.

    I will address responding to CRs and DRs in Chapter 12, and production issues associated with change pages in Chapter 10.

14. *Holding a live test demonstration.* When the government is acquiring very big or very new automated systems, offerors are often required to demonstrate those systems in a live test demonstration, or LTD. The LTD, like a Broadway show, is carefully choreographed and scripted for the government review audience.

15. *Holding oral presentations in addition to or in place of a written proposal.* Today, some government organizations are asking for oral presentations rather than written proposals, while other agencies ask for oral presentations in addition to the written proposal. In either case, the government usually designates the number of people who can participate, and even who those people can be by position—the manager of the proposed program, a contract administrator, or one higher level manager, such as a company president or division manager. Particularly when a stand-up presentation is the sole opportunity to present the proposed solution, it is carefully scripted, practiced, and practiced again.

    I discuss oral presentations in Chapter 11.

16. *Requesting a best and final offer.* After all questions have been answered and all presentations have been made, the government may ask for a *best and final offer,* or BAFO. This is what it sounds like: the offerors' very best bottom-line cost for performing on the contract.

17. *Submitting a best and final offer.* Pricing personnel look at the current state of the proposal and perform their magic, dropping out or pulling in costs to arrive at the best possible number. Though contract pricing is a subject unto itself, I mention the cost volume in general and some aspects of pricing explicitly later in this chapter and in Chapters 10 and 12.

18. *Awarding the contract.* The government awards the contract based on all elements of the proposal, from written document to LTD to BAFO.

19. *Negotiating the contract.* The offeror and government contract personnel hammer out the details of the contract and schedule a date to begin work.

20. *Holding debriefings.* All offerors are entitled to a debriefing with the government. This is a discussion of the evaluation process and the offeror's score in each of the evaluation factors. Chapter 12 will cover debriefings.

The government and offerors can add steps to the beginning or end of this process. Before a draft RFP is released, for example, the government can release a request for information, or RFI, to gather from potential offerors information on the state of the art or the future state of the art in various technical areas that will be represented in the bid. Likewise, at the end of the solicitation, an offeror can protest the bid if that offeror feels that the award was made unfairly for any number of reasons. In the middle of the process, the government can also omit various steps, such as the best and final offer or clarification requests and deficiency reports. Often an award is made solely on the basis of the single, full proposal, which is why the proposal must be considered a final document.

In Chapter 2, I'll discuss two models for developing proposals: the support manager model and the value-added model. If the proposal coordinator is working in value-added mode, a proposal may come onto his radar screen as soon as the marketing staff begins researching and marketing to a potential government customer. Indeed, the value-added proposal coordinator may be responsible for tracking RFPs. If the proposal coordinator is working as a support manager, the proposal is more likely brought to his attention only when the RFP is imminent. In either situation, the proposal coordinator should be familiar with the entire proposal process and understand where a proposal is in that process in order to schedule resources and provide support.

The proposal coordinator should also have more or less of an understanding of the FAR—the rules and regulations that provide the context for RFPs—and the Freedom of Information Act, which allows citizens to request information from the government.

### The Federal Acquisition Regulation

The FAR, available online at www.arnet.gov/far/ and in hard copy from Management Concepts, Inc. (www.managementconcepts.com), lays out the procurement regulations for the federal government. It is the subject of college-level courses for government contractors and is too big to tackle here, but someone in your proposal organization—usually a pricing specialist—should be intimately familiar with the document.

The proposal coordinator—particularly the coordinator who is working in value-added mode, as described in Chapter 2—should also have a general sense of the most important regulations, including those applying to the timing of amendments with respect to the final proposal deadline, cost and pricing data, financial audits, debriefings, and any other pieces of the proposal or the proposal process that could be affected by the regulations. You won't know exactly what those regulations are until you skim the document, looking for sections that could affect you. Once you do, your knowledge—limited as it may be—will serve as a backup to that of the expert so that if that expert is on vacation or involved in another project when a procedural error occurs, you will be in a position to sound an alert and seek expert advice.

Though procedural errors are rare, they do exist. As is true with any other area of work, government contracting agents vary in skills, experience, and temperament. While most government contract employees see their roles as getting the best value for the government through a fair and reasonable process that recognizes the efforts of contractors as partners with the government, a handful of those employees seem to enjoy making the procurement process as painful as possible. Among them are those who toy with the FAR to the advantage of no one. They should be questioned by a knowledgeable counterpart in your company when, for example, they issue an amendment requiring extensive changes without allowing enough time for the contractor to respond to those changes.

I'm guessing that knowledge of the FAR will become more important as Internet postings of RFPs and electronic submissions of proposals become more popular. As I discuss more thoroughly in Chapter 5, Internet posting of RFPs, amendments, and other solicitation documents has added a new dimension to the solicitation process, one that tends to put a responsibility once held by the government into the hands of contractors. As a consequence, contractors will have to be increasingly alert to technological glitches that could disrupt the procurement process and perhaps violate the FAR.

Stay informed.

### The Freedom of Information Act

You might be familiar with the Freedom of Information Act through the news media, who regularly employ this legislation when preparing investigative reports on government activities. FOIA has more mundane uses, however, including finding out what the government is paying for a particular contract and what that contract entails.

Because certain types of contracts tend to repeat themselves while others do not, some industries employ this tool more than others. When you're preparing a proposal to build a new software system, a FOIA request will probably get you nowhere. But when you're preparing a contract for basic software support, a FOIA request might yield results. In general, businesses that can benefit from FOIA requests offer basic operations and maintenance support, such as base operations, call center services, facilities management, janitorial services, software maintenance, and health reviews.

If your company is among those offering basic services, you should have some understanding of the Freedom of Information Act and the reasons that a FOIA officer can turn down a request so that you can argue on behalf of your company should your request be denied. I'll discuss this further in Chapter 5. The point here is to read the document and be prepared.

Now that you see the larger context of proposals, we can move on to the specific: the request for proposals.

## THE REQUEST FOR PROPOSALS

The RFP is the government's standardized document for requesting negotiated bids. I don't pretend to be an expert on all its pieces, and you don't have to be one, either. To be a proposal coordinator, you need to be somewhat familiar with the entire RFP, including attachments, and intimate with Sections C, L, and M. The sections are as follows:

- *Section A: Solicitation/Contract Form.* This is a cover sheet providing summary information on the bid.

- *Section B: Supplies or Services and Prices/Costs.* This is a format for completing the cost proposal, sometimes known as the B tables.

- *Section C: Description/Specification/Work Statement.* This is usually the heart of the specification or statement of work, but attachments can include additional specifications that are integral to the bid.

- *Section D: Packaging and Marking.* This section includes instructions for delivering materials to the government after the contract award. It does not discuss packaging of the proposal itself.

- *Section E: Inspection and Acceptance.* This section contains any special requirements for inspecting and accepting items delivered under the proposed contract.

- *Section F: Deliveries or Performance.* Section F stipulates where the contract will be performed and deliveries made.

- *Section G: Contract Administration Data.* This section contains information on government contracting agents and auditing agencies.

- *Section H: Special Contract Requirements.* Section H is a mish-mash of contract-specific instructions covering indirect and direct costs, key personnel, equipment, property, maintenance, and other items.

- *Section I: General Provisions.* This section lists all federal acquisition and technical standards that are included in the RFP by reference, which means that they must be considered to be part and parcel of the RFP.

- *Section J: List of Documents, Exhibits, and Other Attachments.* Section J is a list of attachments, followed by the attachments themselves. Some of the attachments are specifications, lists of hardware and software, maps, configurations, and certifications.

- *Section K: Representations, Certifications, and Other Statements of Offeror.* This is a standard set of forms that must be completed by the offeror and is usually submitted in the cost proposal.

- *Section L: Instructions, Conditions, and Notices to Offerors or Quoters.* These are specific instructions for organizing and submitting your proposal.

- *Section M: Evaluation Factors for Award.* This section describes how the government will evaluate the proposal.

Within these sections, the contracting organization can include or exclude any number of standardized pieces. Over time, you will notice that any one organization has its preferred sections and forms that are used repeatedly in each RFP that the organization releases. For example, some agencies provide an overview of the work requirements in Section C but the meat of the statement of work in the attachments. Other agencies include background investigation forms, collective bargaining agreements, equipment inventories, or résumé formats in each RFP.

Don't let your expectations lull you into a hypnotic state when you're reading an RFP. A surprise clause can make or break a proposal. Stay alert!

## THE FINAL PRODUCT

The proposal coordinator coordinates the activities of various people to produce a proposal, which consists of a number of documents specified by the government in Section L of the RFP. A representative, generic proposal might include these volumes or sections:

Technical Volume

- Executive Summary

- Technical Approach

- Management Approach

- Past Performance

- Résumés

Cost Volume

- Standard Form 33 and amendment acknowledgments

- Section B—the completed pricing tables

- Pricing Assumptions

- Representations and Certifications

- Bid or Performance Bond.

The government may also ask for any number of other sections or volumes, from a subcontracting plan to a live test demonstration plan.

The specifics of the documents are inconsequential. Generally, the government allows some flexibility of format in volumes or sections that describe a set of products and services and explain how those products and services will be delivered. The government usually prescribes formats for sections on corporate past performance, personnel experience, or cost.

I review the generic sections of a generic proposal below.

## Executive Summary

The executive summary is a (surprise!) summary of all aspects of the proposal at a high level, created for government executives who want to know salient features of the bid without wading through technical details. Rumor has it that when proposal sections are split among reviewers, the executive summary is used to provide all reviewers with an overview of the whole so that each reviewer sees where the section he is reviewing fits. Executive summaries can cover briefly any or all aspects of the technical and management proposals described below.

I've seen executive summaries that were nearly all graphics or nearly all text. I prefer a combination of both, guessing that a mix of text and graphics will please reviewers who are visually oriented and those who are verbally oriented.

Some proposal experts advise their clients to write the executive summary before other parts of the proposal, even before the RFP is released. In my experience, however, only the largest companies have the marketing resources required to identify fully the proposal solution, strategies, themes, and discriminators necessary to formulate an executive summary before the RFP arrives, or even at the beginning of the writing process. For this reason, executive summaries are more likely to be prepared after major sections of the proposal have been developed, and they are updated until the proposal moves into final production.

**Technical and Management Proposals**

Technical and management proposals describe the products and services to be provided, how they will be provided, and what advantages they offer to the customer. Their various sections have evolved to look something like Example 1-1. This model includes the following items:

- *Section headings*. Section headings provide the hierarchical structure for the proposal.

- *Theme statements*. Theme statements summarize the features and benefits of the offeror's proposed products and services relative to a section.

- *Figures*. Figures are graphic representations of some proposed product or service or an aspect of a product or service.

- *Tables*. Tables are sets of columns and rows with headings that can include numerical, text, or graphic information, such as check marks.

- *Action captions*. Action captions summarize features and benefits represented in a figure or table.

- *The proposal narrative*. The proposal narrative is my term for text, exclusive of theme statements and action captions.

Some time back, I received a direct-mail advertisement from a nationally known proposal consultant saying that because the format outlined above with theme statements and action captions has become standard in the industry, offerors are canceling each other out. That is, no offeror stands above the others as an organization having a unique format or different approach to proposals.

His point is well taken, but for the foreseeable future, I think most of us in the business will continue to work with the same standard format because it works. Moreover, my experience says that within this format companies have ample opportunity to shine or flop. All text is not equal; all action captions are not equal; all graphics are not equal.

Formats are, however, loosening up somewhat. In our organization, government proposals are looking more like commercial proposals every day. As color technology has become cheaper, government proposals have become glossier and more colorful. Still, information presented well is what counts, no matter what the structure.

**Example 1-1:** Sample Page Format

---

Shannon Associates                                                      RFP IRS970005

**[Header]**  **[Section]**

SECTION 1: TECHNICAL APPROACH | 1.1.1  Approach to Developing Software

**1.1   Developing, Testing, and Maintaining Software**

*Senior engineers with a combined 400 years of NASA mission experience have adapted Shannon Associates' methodologies for developing, testing, and maintaining from space-tested systems. The result is software with overall reliability, mean time between failure, 99.99% availability, and 10-minute repair or replacement.*

NA **[Theme]** demand software that is more reliable, maintainable, and available than software developed for nearly any other purpose. Clearly, software that fails on the ground or in the air endangers both lives and mission goals.

Shannon Associates **[Figure Title and Action Caption]** ch to developing, testing, a software provides procedure

- Isolate and track the smallest possible units from development through maintenance
- Debug and test using a fully computerized model of the spacecraft
- Pinpoint failed mod **[Table Title and Action Caption]** in utes
- Replace failed module res
- Repair failed modules

These features were designed by senior engineers with long experience on the Hubble Space Telescope, Space Station Freedom, and the Space Shuttle orbiter. These engineers were team leaders in developing mission-critical software for launch, orbit, rend **[Table]** de scent that performed reliably for many years.

As those software systems have been replaced with less cumbersome, modern equivalents, our engineers have adapted the methodologies used with them. Shannon Associates' updated, proven methodologies produce the same reliability with even mo **[Footer]** ail ability and maintainability.

*Shannon Associates designs* **[Figure/Table Callout]** *10-minute replacement or rep- tems are never compromised by software failure.*

Figure 1.1.1-1 illustrates our software development process.

**[Figure]**

**Figure 1.1.1-1. Shannon Associates' Software Development Process.** We design units for replacement or repair in five minutes.

The features and benefits of our process appear in Table 1.1.1-1.

**Table 1.1.1-1. Features and Benefits of the Development Process.** Our approach is proven to provide fast change-out of mission-critical modules.

| Feature | Benefit |
|---|---|
| Requirements gathering covers mechanical, human, and replacement requirements | Failed units are identified, replaced, or repaired in 10 minutes through human-friendly mechanical systems |
| Units are fully designed for replacement before coding | Units are never broken after coding, preserving the unit integrity and preventing errors |
| Units are coded in parallel | If the government wishes, coding can move faster or slower to meet coordinated schedules |

## Résumés and Past Performance

Résumé and past performance portions of the proposal are often highly structured in response to requirements in the RFP. A résumé may look like Example 1-2. An item in the past performance section might resemble Example 1-3.

Preparing these sections often requires more research than writing. The text associated with résumés and past performance must, however, be slanted to highlight aspects of individual or corporate experience that are related to the current bid. This exercise requires some understanding of the work being proposed, the individual or corporate experience described (by an individual or a project representative), and the relationship between the two. This tedious work of sorting out what is and is not relevant and digging to find applicable credentials is often neglected.

**Example 1-2:** Sample Résumé Format

**James Weigand**
**Proposed Position: Program Manager**

**Shannon Associates**                                        **May 1994–Present**

**Position**: Program Manager
**Date**: June 1997–April 2000
**Contract**: MBS 2
**Agency**: Health Administrative Board

**Description**: Managed the contract to develop software for Management Business System (MBS) 2, a set of updates to the MBS system. Hired and supervised 50 programmers, analysts, and clerical staff who developed 10 system upgrades, including financial, administrative, and scheduling programs. Scheduled program milestones, reviewed deliverable documents, and supervised coding, testing, and system maintenance. Programs were written in C, C++, and Fortran.

**Position**: Technical Lead
**Date**: May 1994–June 1997
**Contract**: Independent Data System
**Agency**: Manion Technologies, Inc.

**Description**: Served as a technical lead for a commercial contract to collect and organize corporate financial and management data. Designed and led programming for 15 system components gathering data from five corporate divisions. Oversaw independent testing and one-by-one movement of modules and components from test to operational environments. Worked with technical writers to prepare all system documentation from specifications to user manuals. Used C++ and Oracle forms capabilities.

**Technology Systems, Inc.**                                    **January 1991–May 1994**

**Position**: Lead Programmer
**Date**: November 1991–May 1994
**Contract**: Space Scheduling System
**Agency**: NASA

**Description**: Designed and programmed a system for detailed scheduling of space missions from conception through launch. Collected mechanical, human, and mission requirements; wrote system specifications; and programmed the system using Ada. Developed presentations materials for stand-up reviews and responded to questions from government managers.

## Cost Volume

The cost volume usually includes any or all of these items:

- *Standard Form 33 and Acknowledgments.* A completed form 33—the cover page for the RFP—is normally returned with the cost proposal, along with acknowledgments of amendments. Amendments are acknowledged by completing and signing the cover page of each amendment, Standard Form 30.

**Example 1-3:** Sample Past Performance Format

| | |
|---|---|
| *Contract:* | NYC 100093 |
| *Agency:* | City of New York |
| *Contract Person:* | James T. Johnson |
| *Address:* | Office of Parking Enforcement |
| | 95 Wall Street, New York, New York 10053 |
| *Phone:* | (212) 339-4456 |
| *Contract Start Date:* | May 1994 |
| *Contract Completion Date:* | April 1997 |
| *Original Funding:* | $1,345,000 |
| *Final Funding:* | $1,589.000 |

**Contract Description:** Provided temporary staffing for parking enforcement, administrative, and clerical positions, including parking police, administrative assistants, data entry clerks, and quality check clerks. Gathered position descriptions and criteria as position openings arose, interviewed and hired temporary staff, and tracked staff performance through interaction with the temporary personnel and city managers. The contract was extended beyond the original completion date to allow additional time to select a successor. This extension caused an increase in the total contract funds as noted in the Final Funding row, above.

**Relevance to Current Contract:** The NYC contract is similar to San Diego's staffing contract in that Shannon Associates will again provide temporary staffing in a number of administrative and clerical categories over two years. The methodologies that we describe in this proposal were used on the NYC contract, and several of the senior-level managers being proposed for the current contract were integral to our success there.

- *Prices/Costs*. Section B of the RFP is an outline for pricing the bid that must be completed for the cost volume. Sometimes the government asks for prices on broad categories of services. Sometimes the offeror must provide costs for numerous contract line item numbers (CLINs) and subcontract line item numbers (SLINS) that run page after page, creating an enormous cost volume.

  Additionally, the FAR defines when cost and pricing data in support of the offeror's final pricing are required. Most of the proposals I currently produce are for firm, fixed-price contracts for which cost and pricing data are not required. But occasionally we produce a proposal for a cost plus award fee contract, for which data are required. Cost proposals that include cost and pricing data are far larger, and the copying process is longer.

- *Assumptions, Conditions, or Exceptions*. The government sometimes asks offerors to state assumptions, conditions, or exceptions associated with pricing the bid. Here you provide any numbers you used that were not taken from the government's own price schedules, any conditions that would cause you to change your final cost estimate, and any exceptions to the RFP requirements that have been factored into your cost. For example, if you are predicting the final cost of a product that will be available only next year, you may need to note that this price could change if the product costs more to develop than was originally predicted.

- *Representations and Certifications*. The reps and certs, as they're sometimes called, cover a range of topics relative to your company's status as a contractor and authorize someone in your organization to negotiate with the government. The blank form in Section K of the RFP must be completed for the proposal and is usually submitted in the cost volume.

- *Bid or Performance Bonds*. Some agencies require a bid bond or a performance bond as assurance that your company can complete the work as proposed. These are normally handled through your company's insurance agent. A bid bond amount is often a percentage of the total proposed cost, so the bond cannot be prepared before a target or final cost is identified.

All these sections can appear overwhelming. To make them less so, you need to break them down into manageable parts and reuse material whenever possible. I'll address those issues later.

# CHAPTER 2

# *Understanding the Roles and Environment*

Before you can create an environment that supports a stress-free proposal process, you must examine and understand the proposal coordinator's role, the people he works with, and the conditions under which he works. This understanding will serve you well in negotiating with managers to create a hospitable environment for the success of your process and in assessing your own capability to foster a process that serves you and others.

## THE PLAYERS

On the government side, the solicitation process is shepherded by a *contracting officer* who oversees the procurement from RFP development through contract award, and sometimes through contract implementation. The contracting officer is often assisted by *contract specialists*, who do much of the administrative work of developing a bidders list, posting the RFP to a website or sending it to bidders, or issuing amendments. Contract specialists often act as the liaisons between offerors and contracting officers.

On the contractor side we have a cast of characters that develops and produces proposals. I use the term "developing" to include all the elements included in putting words and pictures on paper: storyboarding, writing, and creating graphics. I use the term "producing" to describe the elements—copyediting, placing graphics, and formatting text—that go into perfecting the document for delivery.

Developing the proposal is the job of the design team—a set of managers and subject-matter experts chosen for their knowledge of the customer or of pertinent technologies, tools, methods, and procedures. The design team is often headed by a *capture manager*. Producing the proposal is the responsibility of the production team, a group of graphic artists, word processors, and copyeditors who are often headed by a *production manager*. The proposal coordinator operates somewhere between the design team and the production team, coordinating activities within and between the teams. I refer to the two groups and the proposal coordinator as the proposal team.

Each proposal team is configured according to the size of the bid, relationships among departments, and staff available. In small companies, the capture manager often develops and produces the proposal with the assistance of limited editorial and production staff. In mid- to large-size companies bidding larger jobs, the capture manager, proposal coordinator, and production manager are normally separate individuals in distinct positions.

Very large companies bidding very large jobs usually assign a capture manager to head an offeror's response to a solicitation from beginning to end; a proposal coordinator to manage development and production of the entire proposal; a volume manager for each volume to coordinate development of that volume; a production manager to supervise production of the entire proposal; and a book manager to coordinate production of an assigned volume or volumes. *"Book Boss" usually means "Vol. Mgr" in Huntsville*

In effect, however, the activities remain the same no matter how big the proposal. A capture manager for a small proposal carries out the steps described here, in addition to other steps associated with developing a technical solution and pricing that solution. A volume manager for a very large proposal is essentially a proposal coordinator for a segment of the document and also performs the activities described here. The proposal coordinator for a very large proposal is a "meta-coordinator" who ensures that each volume manager carries out the steps described here.

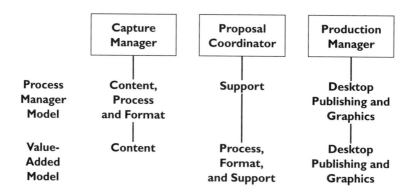

In the mid-sized configuration consisting of the capture manager, proposal coordinator (or proposal manager), and production manager, the proposal team can function in what I call a support manager model or value-added model. I would provide organizational charts showing the differences in the process manager and value-added models, but organizational charts don't really highlight the distinctions, which lie ultimately in who controls the process for developing the proposal and the final form its content will take. In the ~~support~~ *process* manager model, the capture manager is essentially in control of the entire form and content of the proposal and the process for developing it. In the value-added model, the capture manager controls the content; the proposal coordinator controls the form of the content, the process, and the proposal support. The production manager's role remains unchanged in either case. *PROP. MGR. HAS MORE POWER IN THIS ROLE*

In the support manager model, the proposal coordinator fulfills a largely administrative function, with limited attachment to the ultimate outcome. In the value-added model, the proposal coordinator is the ultimate quality control checkpoint for all the text and graphics, the timeline, and the delivery.

The reporting structure is then not as important as the deference the capture manager offers—or doesn't offer—to the proposal coordinator when it comes to form and process, and the respect that the proposal coordinator shows the capture manager regarding the substance of the proposal.

I think the value-added model is clearly the superior of the two for the reason expressed in the judgmental title that I've given to the model: In the value-added model, the proposal coordinator adds more value to the proposal. She improves on the writing, compliance, and look of the product. She also has more control of the process and the product. This is not control merely for the sake of the controlling—to build a proposal empire. It is control to maintain a consistent process, apply institutional memory, and reduce stress for all involved.

With control, however, comes complexity. The proposal coordinator job in the value-added model is far more complex than it is in the process manager model. It involves value judgments on the quality of the writing, the artistic merit of the graphics, and the compliance of the proposal, bit-by-bit and as a whole. It means juggling attitudes and resources to arrive at a balance, as described below.

If you're starting a proposal shop, you'll want to define the type of model you're going to use. If you already have a proposal shop that's not functioning properly, you'll want to examine these models to clarify the model you're using. An inordinate amount of conflict and, consequently, a pileful of stress in the proposal process originate from confusion among the participants about which model they're using and what is expected of each party to the process.

Think of the proposal model as an epicenter of the proposal. Disagreements originating at the epicenter ripple out, disrupting the process and causing frustration and stress to the outer reaches of the process and the organization. When the epicenter is calm, it ceases to be an epicenter, because no earthquake exists.

Calm is what you're seeking.

## THE PROPOSAL COORDINATOR — 2 ROLES: SUPPORT THE TEAM / MANAGE THE PROCESS

In the value-added proposal model, the proposal coordinator is closely involved in supporting the proposal team and managing the proposal process. In the support manager model, the proposal coordinator is less involved in managing the process but has an obvious stake in the outcomes of that process as each of the milestones is reached. If a milestone is missed, the proposal team must get back on track, or the proposal coordinator and production staff must make up for the lost time at the end of the process. Wrapping up the process under a compressed schedule creates stress—not for the design team, but for the production team.

In both models, the proposal coordinator's position involves two inherently different functions: (1) supporting the proposal team administratively and (2) managing the proposal process so that it runs smoothly.

In the support role, the proposal coordinator uses her expertise in the form and substance of winning proposals to facilitate the work of other people. In this role, she provides services to customers, that is, the design teams that cycle through the proposal shop. The team needs various types of support:

- Computer and phone services

- Proposal development instructions and formats

- Review instructions and formats

- Pointers to pertinent material, such as boilerplate or past performance data

- Assistance in negotiating their way through the corporation to obtain material they are lacking

- Word processing support

- Graphics support

- Editorial support.

In the management role, on the other hand, the proposal coordinator actively manages the proposal process by planning and holding meetings and tracking events against a schedule to ensure a predictable outcome. She also ensures compliance with government and corporate requirements by checking the form and content of the proposal against those requirements as it develops.

The dual nature of the proposal coordinator position can be problematic. One role carries with it an attitude of serving people—asking them what they need and giving it to them. The other role is one of expecting and sometimes demanding performance to meet the schedule, government requirements, and proposal standards.

Good proposal coordinators handle both roles well. When setting yourself up for success, you will want to consider each role and develop relationships and processes to carry out that role in a stress-free manner.

### Position Characteristics

The proposal coordinator's two roles are further complicated by several factors. First, he works with individuals who cycle through the proposal shop on temporary assignment. Second, he works with those who outrank him in the corporate hierarchy. Third, he works with numerous other divisions of the company to carry out his mission. Fourth, the proposal coordinator frequently does not manage the proposal budget. I will explore these factors individually.

1. Proposals and proposal teams come and go. Assume that the average turnaround time for a generic proposal from RFP release to proposal submission is between 45 and 60 days, although the turnaround time is frequently shorter. Assume also that your company is regularly bidding contracts. Under this scenario, a different set of individuals passes through the proposal shop some eight times per year.

To grasp the impact of this revolving set of visitors, imagine the same scenario in your home. Imagine that every several months you acquire a new set of roommates with different personalities and habits. One person likes to clean the refrigerator, the next one never empties the kitty litter, and the next one stays up all night and sleeps all day. To adapt, you must either be a very special, go-with-the-flow person or resolve to set some basic ground rules that define your limits.

The proposal coordinator position offers the same opportunity for disorientation and frustration as rotating roommates, for precisely the same reason. Every time a new individual—let alone an entire team of individuals—enters your sphere, you both make adjustments. The question every time is how much adjustment each party is going to make.

If you're going to have a proposal process that works, you, as the keeper of the proposal process, must make sure that your process remains stable while others adjust to it. You might want to allow a little wiggle room to adapt to your visitors, but "little" is the operative word. The more you adapt to others who are temporary visitors in your shop, the less real process remains. Finally, you will have no process at all.

2. The second factor—working with individuals who rank higher in the organization than the proposal coordinator—exacerbates the first factor. In my experience, the capture manager, other members of the proposal team, and reviewers often rank higher in the corporate hierarchy than the proposal coordinator. In today's businesses, these personnel have usually worked with a number of companies, each having its own proposal process (or no process) that may or may not be consistent with your own. Furthermore, they are accustomed to making their own decisions and guiding their own programs. Occasionally, high-ranking visitors take offense when a lower-ranking proposal coordinator tries to realign the agenda to be more in keeping with the established process.

Again, even when confronted by high-ranking individuals with more and different experience, your process must remain stable, or you will end up with no process at all. Here you may need help in establishing ground rules and making them stick, even in the face of visiting dignitaries.

Another factor in both the support role and the management role is that the proposal coordinator works with people who are outside his direct sphere of control to deliver services and to ensure compliance with government and corporate requirements. These individuals may include the following:

- Computer and phone support personnel (who provide extra computers, phones, access codes, and passwords)

- Security staff (who issue name tags and access codes for rooms and buildings)

- Human resources staff (who may provide access to consultants, hold in-house résumés, or provide position descriptions)

- Technical staff (who hold relevant past performance data)

- Contract and cost personnel (who also may have past performance data and the cost data for the current proposal)

- Purchasing departments (who may need to issue purchase orders for people hired or things purchased for proposals).

3. In the management role, the proposal coordinator also oversees the schedules and coordinates the activities of those who work in other divisions for other managers. This necessary reliance on personnel who do not report to the proposal coordinator can be as problematic as working with revolving sets of visitors and working with higher-ranking colleagues.

The proposal coordinator manages processes and schedules, not people (with the possible exception of consultants and production personnel). When performance reviews roll around, he is rarely called upon to evaluate the performance of any members of the proposal team or other personnel he calls on to contribute to the proposal process. He therefore wields little or none of the leverage typically used to sway folks who are underperforming. In worst-case situations, the proposal coordinator position becomes one of great responsibility—sometimes linked to performance-based bonuses or salary increases—with little authority to correct problems that arise. He can use a carrot to encourage quality performance but holds no stick as backup if the carrot doesn't work.

This characteristic of the proposal coordinator's position makes it all the more important to lay the foundation for success by building support from managers inside and outside your division. This may mean asking managers to talk with managers above your level to reach agreements that will affect your life.

## Working without a Budget

Some proposal coordinators are hampered by an additional factor: they are out of the budget loop. In some proposal shops, proposal coordinators don't manage the entire proposal budget or even a limited budget covering the individuals working directly or indirectly for them: writing consultants, word processors, or other support staff.

This puts the proposal coordinator at an added disadvantage for two reasons. First, technical managers who are unfamiliar with the proposal process often underestimate the cost of editorial and production services from the start. I recognized this problem when I was working as a full-time production manager. Pulling together the editorial and production costs by calculating an hourly rate for salaried employees, I arrived at a solid, per-page cost for editing and production. But few managers believed me because they thought the cost was too high! I confirmed the per-page price with proposal after proposal, but I still ran into flat denial that the costs could be accurate. For this reason, I firmly believe that the proposal coordinator must have direct or indirect access to budget development so that the numbers are right from the beginning.

Secondly, cost overruns occurring at the beginning of the process, when the capture manager has greatest influence, tend to have a cumulative effect on the end of the process, when the proposal coordinator has the greatest influence and when the support staff is most involved. If the design team takes more time than expected to arrive at a technical solution, you can find yourself low on money before the back-end processes begin. This can negatively affect your final product by forcing you to omit editing or truncate production. Alternatively, dwindling financial resources can put pressure on editorial and production staff to do their work in less time or work overtime without overtime pay or compensatory time off.

Neither situation is conducive to a good product or process. To prevent overruns that disrupt life, the proposal coordinator should be an expert on proposal costs for labor and material and should have the power to ensure that the end of the process is not shortchanged.

In the best setting and with the best talent, the proposal coordinator position remains unusual, complex, and challenging. The proposal coordinator both supports and manages, juggling both roles to keep the process moving. He also works with a variety of visitors to his shop, many of them senior-level managers, mustering additional resources from across the corporation. In addition, he may or may not have access to a budget that he can control in the service of a good process and product.

With the exception of access to the budget, most of the conditions under which the proposal coordinator works cannot be changed. They are simple facts of the position, for better or worse. After all, there are advantages and disadvantages to the characteristics described above. For example, working with higher-level personnel, while challenging, also offers the proposal coordinator exposure to the highest levels of the corporation, which can be beneficial. Working with various divisions provides the opportunity to develop skills at coordinating and coaxing performance.

The goal of this guide is to understand the job and structure it so that you run it—it doesn't run you. Now that you understand the position, we will explore the corporate and personality characteristics that will affect your performance in that position. Then I'll explain how you can set yourself up for success.

## The Proposal Coordinator's Corporate Setting

Some proposal coordinators are better positioned than others to control their own environments by virtue of their location in the corporate hierarchy. Proposal shops vary greatly. It is in the proposal coordinator's best interests to ferret out the answers to several questions before taking a new job or attempting to alter an established process.

To understand where you are in the vast corporate sea, ask the following questions:

- Is the proposal shop within the business development arm of the organization or under the publications division?

- To whom does the proposal coordinator report?

- What is that person's title?

- What is the salary?

- How are resources allocated during proposal efforts? Are members of proposal teams dedicated to the proposal effort?

- What support mechanisms for proposals are in place? Databases? Libraries? Computers? Production staff?

In my experience, business development divisions are considered critical to the corporate livelihood. Publications divisions are held in lower esteem and treated accordingly. A proposal coordinator within a business development arm usually holds a higher position and can bring greater resources to bear when they're needed, backed by senior managers.

An easy way to establish a proposal shop's position in the corporation is to identify the position of the highest manager. Managers of business development divisions are frequently vice presidents, senior vice presidents, or executive vice presidents. Managers of publications units rarely hold these executive positions.

If you're going to hold your own with the senior managers who cycle through your shop, maintaining your process and your sanity, you want to be positioned where the power is.

Another aspect of the marketing department versus publications department conundrum that is increasingly affecting proposal departments is the attempt to merge the proposal coordinator role with that of the production manager in the new corporate environment. *GRAPHICS SKILLS + EXPERIENCE INCREASINGLY A PART OF THE PROP. MANAGER JOB DESCRIPTION*

Increasingly, publication tools are available on each desktop in the corporation, usually in the form of Microsoft Office components, such as Microsoft® Word and PowerPoint®. This fact has been a boon to staff, who can produce small documents with simple graphics quickly and without secretarial support. It is typically a bust for the proposal process.

First, typical desktop products in a Windows environment are not designed for large desktop publishing tasks. Building and manipulating graphics in such programs remains difficult and cumbersome. Second, involving the proposal coordinator too closely in the production process takes that person away from the quality control role that he should be playing, particularly in the value-added model. As is true with any type of work, you cannot provide quality control for work that you yourself have performed. Everyone—particularly a person under deadline pressure—needs another set of eyes to check the work. The proposal coordinator should provide that set of eyes, while another person or set of persons actually produces the document.

Salary is a good predictor of authority. It is also a good measure of how much a company values your services, and I have little use for companies who don't pay for proposal development experience. It's one thing to work for a start-up company, where all staff are sacrificing some element of comfort (security, high salary, nights and weekends) to participate in an exciting new venture. It's another thing to be the only staff member among technical and marketing personnel who lags in compensation.

Proposal coordinators have a particular set of skills—and normally an appropriate set of degrees—that are not duplicated among technical and marketing staff. If a company doesn't offer the proposal coordinator a salary equivalent to that of subject-matter experts or marketing personnel with equal experience, you will probably be poorly positioned to create a workable proposal process. You will probably also find that it's almost impossible to catch up if you begin with a salary that is below that of your colleagues.

Also beware of performance-based bonuses that purport to make up for low salaries if the only way you can achieve the bonus is to overwork yourself or your staff. If you don't have the authority and backing to create a winning proposal in a stress-free environment, that bonus amounts to overtime pay with no time-and-a-half differential. Bonuses are also problematic if they are linked solely to your win rate because of the extent to which costs affect wins or losses. You could write fully compliant proposals that are coupled with overly high or overly low costs and lose every one. Weigh bonuses carefully.

## Corporate Allocation of Resources

A good salary and appropriate authority will do little for you if you don't have the resources you need. In one consulting stint at a well-known corporation, I noticed that all the design team members were working full-time on contracts while they were also preparing the proposal. Not one of the principal team members was dedicated entirely to the proposal effort.

Even if you wield ample authority, this is a proposal coordinator's nightmare, simply because one can demand only so much from a set of individuals. If the demands of current customers always come first for every individual on the design team, you are bound to find yourself slipping deadlines and backing off from holding individuals to their commitments.

Companies tend to exhibit trends in allocation of human resources for proposals—either they consistently do or consistently do not. A proposal coordinator may be able to manage an occasional proposal working with "moonlighting" staff, but if a prospective employer always follows this procedure, the signals say look elsewhere.

## Support Resources

Databases, libraries, computers, and production support are signs of a mature organization with processes and procedures in place. If the proposal coordinator is not the direct supervisor of the individuals who provide these support functions, he will want to know how those resources are shared, requested, and delivered and whether or not his requests are considered high priority.

I recall a children's song that goes something like this: "If you can't get over it, go under it; if you can't go under it, go around it." I don't recall the actual point of the song, but it seems to apply here. The proposal coordinator's position has built-in obstacles to success that aren't found in many other corporate positions. He needs to find a way over, under, around, or directly through the middle. Hold this in mind as you consider the personal factors that influence your ability to produce a winning proposal in a stress-free environment.

## Your Personality and Priorities

The proposal coordinator who wants to win proposals in a stress-free environment must be willing to wield all the power afforded to him. In this regard, some personality characteristics get in the way of developing a successful proposal process.

If you enjoy being a martyr who stays up all night to save the proposal from disaster so that others will recognize your company loyalty or diligence, a smoothly running proposal process might limit your opportunities to shine. If you are familiar with mopping up after messes because you're a caretaker by nature, a nicely oiled proposal machine may detract from your *raison d'être*. Ask yourself the following questions:

- Why do you want to be a proposal coordinator? What does the position offer you? A good salary? The opportunity to use editorial and coordination skills? The opportunity to manage people?

- What personal characteristics could get in your way in your role as proposal coordinator? Perfectionism? Fear of people in positions of authority? Insecurity about your capabilities?

- Where do you want the proposal coordinator position to take you? Do you want to stay in the position until you retire? Do you want to use the position as a stepping stone to a higher-level managerial job?

If you're planning to stay in the proposal coordinator position until you retire, you will probably have a different agenda from the person who wants to use the position as a stepping stone to another position. The latter may be willing to put in two years of 12-hour days to ensure the next career step. The proposal coordinator who is in it for the long haul probably doesn't want to continue that grueling schedule.

To create a working proposal process, the proposal coordinator must interact and negotiate with all levels of the corporate hierarchy as a person among equals. This doesn't mean that you ignore any hierarchical structure that exists; rather, it means that you can't buckle when facing a person of greater authority, because most people who enter your sphere will have greater authority than you do, including capture managers, technical leads, and reviewers.

Don't assume that personality characteristics are fixed quantities that can't change. Simply realize that if you want to create a workable process for producing winning proposals in a stress-free environment, you may need to work around or on your personality so you don't stand in your own way. And when you set yourself up for success, you may want to ask colleagues for support so that you are looking out for each others' best interests. The next chapter provides suggestions on how to do this.

# CHAPTER 3

# Setting the Stage for Success

Any proposal coordinator in her right mind wants to build and sustain a proposal process that supports the company in winning new contracts while supporting the people who contribute to the process in having workable lives inside and outside the office.

Many factors in the life of the proposal coordinator work against this goal. Some of these are associated with her roles, environment, and personality. Others are associated with the attitudes described later in this chapter. And some of these things can't be changed. Few companies can afford to create a proposal shop with its own computer support personnel, for example. No one can change the fact that capture managers and proposal teams cycle through the proposal shop, bringing with them attitudes and methods that can be destructive to a successful proposal process.

Some things can be changed, however. In fact, they must be changed if you're going to reach the goal of winning without stress. Change can come from the ground up, but it happens more quickly if it comes from the bottom up and the top down at the same time. To change from both directions, you must enroll your managers in creating a workable process *because it is* a workable process and nothing else is an adequate substitute.

## ENROLLING MANAGEMENT

The statistics are out there. Companies with formal processes for qualifying bids and developing proposals have a substantially higher win rate than companies that go about proposals haphazardly. Part of this success can be attributed to careful selection of the contracts to bid, which is usually handled by marketing personnel. The other part lies in using a consistent process that proposal staff and teams can master over time. This is your job, and you need your managers to support you if you're going to do it right.

If your proposal process is to remain stable as various capture managers and design teams cycle through the proposal shop, you need management concurrence on several points:

- *That your company wants to produce winning proposals in a stress-free environment.* This is a no-brainer. If your managers don't support your goal, they won't support the steps you must take to achieve it.

I hate to admit this, but I'm inclined to believe that you can't convince some managers that this is an admirable goal. We've got two countervailing trends in today's business climate: the frenzied workaholism of start-ups and the move to create family-friendly corporations. Government contractors and other types of commercial enterprises seem to be aligning themselves with either corner: the 24/7 gangs for whom 10 hours a day is a part-time work schedule, or the family-friendly environments, in which love, marriage, children, and parents are acknowledged and taken into account.

People seem to align themselves with one or the other culture and often can't be budged. Moreover, solid proof that proposals are better when produced under less stress is hard to come by in any single organization. The limited available statistics showing that companies with a consistent proposal process have a higher win rate apply to government contracts as a whole.

Consequently, the best tactic for convincing a manager of your high-win, low-stress purpose is to avoid the need altogether by interviewing your manager on the subject before you take a job. If you're already in a job, you'll need to collect general statistics (try the Association of Proposal Management Professionals) and accumulate examples of good and bad proposals. Collecting examples of bad proposals is not a pleasant task, because you'll need to confront your own worst work and offer it up as the worst type of example. Then again, sometimes your worst work confronts you.

I recently produced three proposals in succession. I was exhausted going into the third proposal and tried to beg out, but there was no one to take my place. The resulting proposal—which included an oral presentation—was riddled with minor but embarrassing errors. Because the proposal could not be changed between the hard copy submission date and the stand-up presentation, the oral presentation team was forced to throw my errors up on the screen for the source selection authority to see. I was horrified, they were embarrassed, and my manager saw it all.

Believe me, I did not create these errors to make a point, because I have a phobia of being publicly humiliated. But they are a tremendous example of what an overly tired proposal coordinator can produce, and they made an impact on my manager. Ostensibly, we lost that bid because of a substantial cost differential, but you won't convince me or my boss that those typos made no difference. We were touting ourselves as the *crème de la crème*, while our presentation suggested sour milk.

- *That the process must remain stable, give or take minor adjustments for compelling reasons, such as government requirements.* Using slides, standard forms, and sample instructions, show your manager what the proposal process will be and what roles each of the major participants will play.

Equate the proposal process to other standardized methodologies in your field of business. Nearly every discipline has some type of methodology. Software companies use rigid methodologies for developing and maintaining software; general contractors use standardized methodologies for scheduling and executing construction work; consulting companies employ reengineering methodologies to redesign work processes; and research institutions, accountants, engineering companies, and architecture firms all use some set of standard procedures. These methodologies were designed so that all the checks and balances required to produce a predictable product are in place. Methodologies typically evolve (or are replaced by newer, better methodologies) over time, but a methodology doesn't change because a new program manager takes over the project unless the old methodology is not working.

Research established proposal methods—Shipley (www.shipleywins.com) comes to mind—and see where your methods overlap. You don't need to agree with any standard method, but you want to use the method to substantiate your point: The proposal process cannot change, even if the president of the company serves as the capture manager.

Investigate ISO 9000, Total Quality Management, and Continuous Process Improvement—all catchwords for various types of processes that ensure predictable outcomes. Look at the proposal process objectively as a manufacturing process, with raw materials on one end and a finished product on the other end. Ask yourself what it takes to get from the beginning to the end with quality results. Define what quality means to you. What are the essential components of a winning proposal in your company?

Present the results to your manager with assurance, then ask her to take it to the next level of the corporate structure. My current manager, for example, meets weekly with vice presidents of other divisions. He is in a position to present the overall process to other division managers, explain the process and goals, and influence the outcome of proposals. This step is invaluable in setting the stage for success.

- *That the proposal shop must receive reliable assistance from the other divisions on which it depends.* The proposal coordinator cannot expect to pick up the phone and demand immediate assistance from computer support personnel or human resources staff. She should, however, be able to plan the support needed, negotiate its delivery, and expect cooperation from other divisions in ways that allow the schedule to remain intact.

Ask for your manager's blessing in creating workable relationships with divisions that support or contribute to proposals. If formal, manager-to-manager steps must be taken before you go to other divisions seeking their support, ask your manager to take them within a stipulated time frame.

Then build on those relationships by meeting with the people who will make your life easier, as I will discuss later in this chapter.

- *That the proposal team must be willing and able to meet the proposal schedule without substantial overtime.* If the company wants to produce winning proposals without stress, managers must be committed to supplying the resources needed.

Human resources must be capable, interested, and not overbooked with other projects. One organization I know could not find a permanent position for a staff member, so they assigned him to proposal after proposal, preparing résumés and past performance data. Though the man was very sweet, he lacked writing talent, and his proposal contributions were half-hearted at best. Just any resource will not do.

If you're in a company that is resource-strapped, as many are, obtain without guilt your manager's permission to take time off, recognizing that occasionally this will leave you understaffed. Then make sure you have reliable temporary resources to fill in the gaps. Believe it or not, if you have a solid proposal process in place, there are freelance consultants available who can step into nearly any position, even capture manager, proposal coordinator, or production manager.

Show your manager how time off contributes to production by refreshing employees and improving their performance. Get permission to implement recognition programs and inexpensive rewards that trickle down to the lowest support and production levels, congratulating production staff or computer support personnel on their contribution to your process.

Work with your manager to move unmotivated personnel out of the proposal process (over time, if necessary) and to improve the skills of people who are motivated but unskilled. Make sure that the positions under your control lead somewhere in the organization—that they're not dead-end streets for the employees in them—because dead-ends dampen enthusiasm. Build training for editing classes or software courses into the department budget, making sure that employees continue to improve their skills.

- *That reviewers will be willing and able to take adequate time for review of proposal documents.* Reviews are seldom given the time and attention required, and they won't be unless managers acknowledge the value of reviews. Your manager might not be able to dictate the amount of time that a visiting reviewer devotes to reviewing a proposal, but she may be able to influence that time.

Point out that the "little is better than nothing" approach to reviews often doesn't work. A reviewer who reads and makes changes to one section without reading the whole proposal might be introducing changes that will launch the proposal into chaos. It is your job as proposal coordinator to protect against this; it's your manager's job to support you.

- *That managers will be willing to intercede if the proposal coordinator has exhausted all reasonable options for remaining on schedule and within the established process.* Corporations are not democratic, and some people have much more power than others. If the proposal process is to work, your manager must be willing to intercede when necessary.

Of course, you don't want to be in a position where your manager has to rescue you. This is nearly fatal in the corporate world. Having to be rescued makes you look weak, like you can't handle your own fights. If you're clear on the proposal model you're using, if everyone knows his role, and if the goal is clear and everyone agrees with it, your manager should never have to step in. But as a last resort on an important proposal, your manager should be willing to clarify the issues if you can't.

If you have any suspicion that agreements will be forgotten as soon as they are made, write the agreements down in the form of a contract, listing what you will provide and what your manager will provide. If the agreement is broken by either party, look closely at where it was broken, what happened, and whether the agreement was valid in the first place. Make sure that your manager actually supports your goals and is not just paying lip service to get you off her back.

Keep in mind that you are asking your manager to support you in creating a workable proposal process, but *you* must do the work to make it happen. If you expect your manager to protect you from senior managers who pass through your shop, to make sure your shop works well with the other divisions, or to rescue you from yourself, you can bet that the manager will soon tire of the effort and will trade you for someone who is more self-sufficient.

## Working with Visiting Personnel

When you have obtained agreement from your own manager, you are in a position to indoctrinate other managers who enter the proposal realm in the components of your process. You do this at the proposal planning meeting with individual capture managers and at the kickoff meeting, discussed in Chapter 7.

If your managers support you, you can also arrange to brief senior division managers of organizations that regularly make bids through your shop as a group or individually. Anything that you can do to prepare persons for procedures that they will eventually encounter will contribute to a successful process.

## Working with Senior Managers

Senior managers can serve as capture managers, members of the design team, and proposal reviewers. Issues of power usually don't arise with senior managers if the capture manager's and proposal coordinator's roles are clearly defined; if all personnel are held to the established schedule; and if senior reviewers can act responsibly in their review roles. Making those things happen is no easy matter, and it takes a full commitment to producing winning proposals in a stress-free environment. Furthermore, it demands a strong focus on the process as necessary to the creation of winning proposals.

Some managers may not care whether or not a process is stress-free, but they do care about the corporate bottom line: winning contracts. When you speak with high-level managers, focus on this goal, reminding them that companies with consistent proposal processes have a higher win rate. A consistent proposal process includes a hard-and-fast schedule and constructive reviews.

Also, make sure that you have a clear understanding of who is doing what. Examples 3-1 and 3-2 provide outlines of responsibilities that divide tasks between the proposal coordinator and capture manager for the support manager model and the value-added model so that each person works according to his personal style without disrupting the proposal process. Any model that you develop is fine, providing that the roles are clear.

**Example 3-1:** A Workable Delineation of Responsibilities (Value-Added Model)

*GREATER ROLE FOR PROP. MGR*

| Proposal Coordinator's Responsibilities | Capture Manager's Responsibilities |
|---|---|
| Reviews the budget and reallocates resources in consultation with the capture manager | Develops and tracks the proposal budget |
| Develops and tracks the proposal schedule | Reviews the proposal schedule, making changes in consultation with the proposal coordinator |
| Develops the proposal outline | Reviews the proposal outline, making changes in consultation with the proposal coordinator |
| Develops a compliance and assignment matrix | Makes writing assignments for the assignment matrix and assigns the number of pages per section |
| Develops and presents kickoff materials covering the proposal process and compiles supplementary material for handout | Develops and presents kickoff materials covering the customer, the team, and the bid |
| Facilitates the proposal process by providing workspace support, forms, formats, configuration control, instructions, etc. | Supports the process by ensuring that the team uses forms, formats, configuration control, instructions, etc. |
| Coordinates proposal design team meetings in consultation with the capture manager | Heads the proposal design team meetings and directs work |
| Facilitates the storyboard process by providing forms, instructions, and on-site support | Leads design aspects of the storyboard process by assisting technical and management personnel in formulating the proposal solution |
| Facilitates development of themes and discriminators, features and benefits, theme statements, and action captions | Leads the technical design team in developing themes and discriminators, features and benefits, and action captions |
| Oversees completion of non-cost items in the cost proposal, such as representations and certifications | Leads the pricing team in developing contract costs for the cost volume |
| Critiques the proposal with reviewers to ensure good writing, complete responses, and adherence to the proposal outline | Critiques the proposal with reviewers to ensure good writing, complete responses, and adherence to the proposal outline |
| Reviews the list of reviewers to ensure that all proposal topics are covered | Selects reviewers |

| | |
|---|---|
| Facilitates the review process by providing materials, instructions, and on-site support for the review team | Supports the review process by providing adequate resources and time for the review |
| Brings up issues relative to review comments and proposal compliance | Makes final decisions on which review comments will be incorporated into the document |
| Ensures proposal compliance | Ensures proposal compliance |
| Tracks resources to ensure their appropriate distribution in areas of expertise; ensures that personnel meet their commitments through management agreements | Manages resources to ensure their appropriate distribution in areas of expertise; ensures that personnel meet their commitments |
| Oversees proposal production directly or indirectly | Approves production items, such as the proposal cover, spines, and tabs |
| Assembles and reviews the final document before reproduction | Signs off on the final document before reproduction |
| Checks the proposal page by page | Ensures that the proposal is checked page by page |

If a senior staff member is consistently negligent in meeting agreements, you might begin to correct the situation by asking if you can provide support in some way. Look for a win-win solution, such as providing word-processing support, writing assistance, or relief from part of the assignment. If this doesn't work, turn to the capture manager and, finally, to your own manager.

As in all cases of individuals who are not performing up to snuff, focus on the process rather than the person. Point out that you are willing to do whatever is necessary (shy of overworking yourself or other staff) to make up for poor performance on another person's part. Have backup resources ready. Negotiate, but not at the expense of yourself or your staff.

**Example 3-2:** A Workable Delineation of Responsibilities (Support Manager Model)

| Proposal Coordinator's Responsibilities | Capture Manager's Responsibilities |
|---|---|
| Reviews the budget and reallocates resources in consultation with the capture manager | Develops and tracks the proposal budget |
| Develops and tracks the proposal schedule | Reviews the proposal schedule, making changes in consultation with the proposal coordinator |
| | Develops the proposal outline |
| | Develops a compliance and assignment matrix |
| | Makes writing assignments for the assignment matrix and assigns the number of pages per section |

*LESSER ROLE FOR PROP. MGR.* (handwritten annotation)

| | |
|---|---|
| Develops and presents kickoff materials covering the proposal process and compiles supplementary material for handout | Develops and presents kickoff materials covering the customer, the team, and the bid |
| Facilitates the proposal process by providing workspace support, forms, formats, configuration control, instructions, etc. | Supports the process by ensuring that the team uses forms, formats, configuration control, instructions, etc. |
| | Coordinates proposal design team meetings in consultation with the capture manager |
| | Heads the proposal design team meetings and directs work |
| Facilitates the storyboard process by providing forms, instructions, and on-site support | Leads design aspects of the storyboard process by assisting technical and management personnel in formulating the proposal solution |
| | Leads the technical design team in developing themes and discriminators, features and benefits, and action captions |
| Oversees completion of non-cost items in the cost proposal, such as representations and certifications | Leads the pricing team in developing contract costs for the cost volume |
| | Critiques the proposal with reviewers to ensure good writing, complete responses, and adherence to the proposal outline |
| | Selects reviewers |
| Facilitates the review process by providing materials, instructions, and on-site support for the review team | Supports the review process by providing adequate resources and time for the review |
| | Makes final decisions on which review comments will be incorporated into the document |
| | Ensures proposal compliance |
| Tracks resources to ensure their appropriate distribution in areas of expertise; ensures that personnel meet their commitments through management agreements | Manages resources to ensure their appropriate distribution in areas of expertise; ensures that personnel meet their commitments |
| Oversees proposal production directly or indirectly | Approves production items, such as the proposal cover, spines, and tabs |
| Assembles and reviews the final document before reproduction | Signs off on the final document before reproduction |
| Checks the proposal page by page | Ensures that the proposal is checked page by page |

## ENROLLING OTHER DIVISIONS

If you are highly reliant on other divisions of the company— for example, computer support, human resources, or purchasing—to contribute pieces to the proposal process, it is in your best interest to hold face-to-face meetings with the managers of those divisions to negotiate the terms and conditions for support. Ask for your own manager's blessing before doing so, then work your way through the managers of divisions that might support or detract from your process.

Make this an ongoing affair rather than a one-time deal. Pull other divisions into the process so they can see where they fit in the overall scheme of things. Give them a better understanding of your purpose in the corporation.

As I write this, I'm thinking of the corporation where I currently work. I have been trying for the past month to restore files damaged by the newest e-mail virus, which infects JPEG files, a digital photograph format. The computer support personnel clearly don't understand why we maintain such a large library of JPEG files and how we put them to use. If they did, I can't imagine that the restoration process would be taking so much time. Obviously, I have not done my job in educating the support managers in what we do and the resources we need to do it.

Share with each manager your goal of creating winning proposals in a stress-free environment. Then ask each for suggestions on how this might be done within the standard operating procedures of that division. Ask the following:

- What kind of lead time do division staff need?

- What procedures should be followed to ask for support?

- Does the division use any standard forms for requesting support?

- Does the division use any standard automated systems you should know about for storing résumés, ordering supplies, etc.?

Consider creating what is known as a service level agreement, a written contract that designates how services will be provided, the process for providing them, and the response time.

## MANAGING YOURSELF

I recently read a best-selling book by a physician who runs a health center in New England. Because she is committed to leading a balanced life *and* sometimes stresses herself and her family in caring for her patients, she asks colleagues at the clinic to question her when she volunteers for extra on-call duty. This small support from her colleagues opens up the opportunity to pause, reflect, and change her mind. She returns the favor by supporting her colleagues in leading balanced lives and accepting extra responsibility only when they are fully willing to do so.

This is a great example of a person and a team setting themselves up for success. If you have tendencies to take the load off others by putting it on yourself, you're a good candidate for such support from one or more colleagues.

Optimally, the supportive colleague should be someone at the same corporate level who is committed to the same outcomes that you are. Another proposal coordinator would be a likely candidate, as would a production manager, if you work with one. Production departments tend to suffer most from slipped deadlines. Production managers should support methods for handling problems without taking on burdens that rightly belong to someone else.

As you create this support network, remember that emergencies do arise, and colleagues sometimes need to rescue each another when they occur. When emergencies are the exception rather than the rule, most of us willingly jump to assist. When emergencies are the rule, most of us develop big chips on the shoulder from carrying resentment.

## MANAGING THE BUDGET

You will note in Examples 3-1 and 3-2 that my models for distribution of responsibility between the capture manager and the proposal coordinator provide the proposal coordinator with an opportunity to review the proposal budget and make changes in consultation with the capture manager. Understanding and approving the budget is critical to a successful proposal process because, through the budget, you can ensure that the resources you control directly or indirectly are not underfunded.

So that you can readily estimate how much support a proposal will need, collect costs from several past proposals. These could be all costs for services from individuals under your supervision, such as consultants, word processors, or graphic artists. They could also cover products such as covers, tabs, spines, paper, pencils, or computer rentals. Whatever framework you choose, count all the charges associated with the proposal, count the pages in that proposal, and arrive at a per-page cost for the past proposals. If you sometimes use proposal development consultants and sometimes don't, prepare estimates with and without consultants. Make sure you are using the fully loaded charge for services that you will be using, as if you were bidding a contract to a client. Fully loaded charges include salary, benefits, and any overhead charges associated with facilities, computers, etc.

Complete this exercise for several past proposals so that you can arrive at a safe estimate of the per-page cost of the proposal. Then ask the capture manager for an estimate of the number of pages for the current proposal and multiply that number by your per-page estimate to arrive at a final estimated cost. If the money budgeted for your services is short of your final estimated cost, you will probably find yourself or others on your staff overworking to make up the difference.

Keep in mind that it is not unusual for companies to underestimate sorely the cost of basic services, such as word processing and graphics support. Eight years ago when I was bidding coordination, editorial, word processing, and graphics support services, my per-page number was $150.00. Again and again, I managed jobs that confirmed this number. Still, when I shared the figure with other experienced consultants in the field, they thought it was way too high. I can only imagine that these folks were not paying attention.

One of your secondary jobs is to educate other managers about the costs of your services and products so that their estimates will be realistic. Even modest proposals in some industries can cost upward of $50,000 when all costs are figured. This expense makes winning all the more imperative.

When you've set yourself up for success by negotiating with managers, developing a support network for yourself, and taking steps to gain control and understanding of the budget, you can address the overriding attitudes about proposals that infiltrate even the best of proposal shops.

## REDEFINING THE CHAOS MENTALITY

One aspect of corporate proposals deserving special attention is the "chaos mentality." In corporate folklore and in actuality, proposals are almost uniformly defined as chaos. In most companies, the more horrific the war story, the better the entertainment value and the higher the badge of honor for living through the experience. The more all-nighters pulled, the more stars on your medal.

Those coming up through the corporate ranks quickly absorb the implied message that the more anxiety-ridden the process is, the better the proposal will be. Accompanying the stories is a hazing-like attitude that goes something like, "I went through it, so you must go through it."

Is it any wonder then that proposals live down to our worst expectations?

If you want to produce winning proposals in a stress-free environment, this attitude has got to go, and pronto. Funny as they may be after the fact, war stories and the accompanying "you gotta live through it" attitude send the wrong message to up-and-coming proposal contributors. Though stories may build short-term camaraderie, they also impede development of a truly productive proposal process and long-term quality contributors by sending the subtle message that deadlines are meaningless and time served equates with quality.

Proposal coordinators would do well to button their lips before the war stories begin and interrupt others with loud coughing. And while you're at it, eliminate other conflict-based terms—such as the "war room"—from the proposal vocabulary. Every time the term "war room" is used, I picture General Douglas MacArthur pacing, puffing on his pipe, and pointing out strategic targets to a room of uniformed men. While acknowledging that proposals are serious business, you want to encourage creativity and productivity—not war. Real war is hell, chaos—all those things you don't want your proposal process to be.

Once the proposal coordinator redefines chaos out of the process and defines proposal development as a set of steps with goals and activities, he can rearrange those steps to suit various proposal teams and to make life easier for himself and his support staff. When he sets the right tone and persistently carries it through, he's on the way to success.

# CHAPTER 4

# Establishing a Proposal Process

*TRACKING RFPs & ANY AMENDMENTS IS PART OF THE PROPOSAL MANAGER'S JOB.*

No one has a sure-fire process for producing successful proposals. Some people use storyboards; some use detailed outlines. Some people edit online; others edit on hard copy. Some people don't edit at all. (Aaaack!) Throughout this guide, I offer my opinions about what works best for me, but my opinions are not sacred. The specific process used is not as important as *having a process and employing it* so that the proposal coordinator and related staff perform a set of activities that can be mastered over time and all members of the proposal team can meet a clear set of objectives.

With that in mind, a proposal process can consist of some or all the following steps:

- *Tracking the RFP and amendments.* When I started this book two years ago, I would have said that tracking the RFP and amendments is a part of the marketing function that is independent of the proposal function. Not anymore. The point when you become aware that an RFP has been released is now entirely in the hands of the government contractor—not the government—and can very much affect the proposal coordinator's operations. Until a better solution is devised, I think that the person who has the most to lose from losing track of the RFP and amendments should have responsibility for their tracking. I say a great deal more about this topic in Chapter 5.

- *Holding a bid/no-bid meeting.* Once the proposal coordinator gets involved in the pre-proposal process, she needs to be tangentially involved in the bid/no bid decision—the corporate decision to plunge ahead or drop a solicitation. I'll say a few words on this subject in Chapter 5.

- *Submitting a Freedom of Information Act request.* This is a front-end part of the proposal process that may or may not be in your line of responsibility. You'll want to develop a standard FOIA letter, which I also discuss in Chapter 5.

- *Holding pre-proposal planning sessions.* With the capture manager and the production manager, the proposal coordinator plans the support and schedule for the upcoming proposal. The pre-proposal planning sessions are described more explicitly in Chapter 7.

- *Outlining the proposal and creating a compliance matrix.* The proposal coordinator outlines the proposal for compliance with Sections C, L, and M of the RFP and any other pertinent specifications, creating a compliance matrix. This process is also discussed in Chapter 7.

- *Attending the pre-bid conference/submitting questions.* The design team generates a set of questions to submit to the government, and a subset of the team attends the pre-bid conference to obtain more background information on the RFP. This conference and the questions are discussed in Chapter 7.

- *Holding a kickoff meeting.* A kickoff meeting, which brings together the entire design team to establish a common understanding of the proposal's premises and processes, is the single most important activity in the proposal process. Don't neglect it. See Chapter 7 for more on this topic.

- *Generating win themes and discriminators.* The proposal coordinator and others, as appropriate, generate a set of win themes and discriminators that will distinguish your company from competitors. This topic is addressed further in Chapter 8.

- *Developing storyboards.* The design team develops a set of storyboards with pictures and themes that will form the core of the proposal. An example of a storyboard appears in Sample A at the end of the book. Storyboards are among the subjects discussed in Chapter 8.

- *Reviewing storyboards.* The design team or a set of independent reviewers comment on the storyboards, adding pertinent suggestions and recommendations. I talk about the storyboard review and the reviews described below in Chapter 9.

- *Writing the Pink Team draft.* The design team writes and the proposal coordinator compiles a rough draft of the proposal.

- *Holding the Pink Team review.* A set of independent reviewers reads and comments on the Pink Team draft, making recommendations to writers and redirecting sections that are moving in the wrong direction.

- *Writing the Red Team draft.* The design team writes and the proposal coordinator compiles a more detailed draft of the proposal.

- *Holding the Red Team review.* A set of independent reviewers reads and comments on the Red Team draft, providing specific suggestions and recommendations for improvements relative to proposal compliance and marketing strategy.

- *Writing the final draft.* The writers integrate the Red Team comments and massage text to create the final document.

- *Producing the proposal.* The production staff copyedits, formats, prints, binds, and packages the document according to Section L specifications. Production issues are discussed in Chapters 6 and 10.

- *Delivering the proposal.* The proposal coordinator packages and mails or hand-delivers the proposal to the location specified in the RFP. Caveats are offered in Chapter 12.

- *Cleaning up after the proposal.* I've added this as a final step to the proposal process because, like many proposal coordinators, I neglect the cleanup. I don't delete files that are no longer useful or update the boilerplate if I've just created the best past performance section that reviewers have ever set eyes on. I'll give you details in Chapter 12. Do as I say, not as I do.

For the proposal coordinator, the proposal process also includes day-to-day management and support activities, but, aside from status meetings, many of these activities are hidden from the proposal team. They take place before the design team arrives or while the team is present, making the process run smoothly.

Before your design team arrives, you should know exactly what your process is, you should have taken any steps addressed in Chapter 3 to smooth the way for that process, and you should have created all of the support forms, formats, and systems discussed here.

## TRACKING THE RFP AND PROPOSAL AMENDMENTS

As I mentioned above, although the Internet has revolutionized the process for issuing RFPs, the result is not pretty. The state of the art is a hodgepodge of websites, each handling RFPs in a different manner, some with e-mail notification, some without, and each demanding the contractor's attention day after day, week after week.

*This has become more standardized as of 2008*

Many of these websites are not ready for prime time, and many of the contracting specialists who deal with them have given over their responsibilities to the Webmasters, preferring to remain clueless as to the ramifications of what they are doing from the contractor's perspective.

This would not be a problem to proposal coordinators if we could just push it off on the marketing staff, but I don't think we can. The way that the government now releases RFPs and amendments seriously affects the proposal process. If we become aware of an amendment several days after it is issued, our entire schedule is thrown off track.

Furthermore, the method that the government uses to release an RFP or amendment has tremendous ramifications on our ability to be responsive. Several days ago, for example, I downloaded an RFP that had been posted as a PDF file for reading and printing in Adobe Acrobat®. The pagination of the file was entirely off, going through a series of low numbers (10, 11, 12, 13), then jumping to higher numbers (56, 57, 58), and back to low numbers. At first I thought that the support staff had bungled the copying, but before I issued accusations, I visited the website and pulled up the file myself. There I found all the jumbled pages on the screen, just as they had been printed.

The point of this raving is that proposal coordinators, who ultimately suffer the consequences of scrambled RFPs, need to interact with contracting specialists and voice their concerns loudly about the current state of Internet postings. For this reason, we need to be involved in the process of tracking proposals on the Internet and must understand how things are happening as they happen. This subject deserves its own chapter, Chapter 5. Freedom of Information Act requests are addressed in the same chapter because they are time-sensitive and need to be submitted early in the tracking process, where possible.

## CREATING MEETING, STORYBOARD, AND REVIEW SUPPORT MATERIALS

Part of the proposal coordinator's role is supporting the proposal team; part of his management role is facilitating the process and guiding the team in using it. This is a matter of demonstrating through formats, forms, graphics, and instructions.

The materials that support the proposal team in a general way are described in Chapters 5 and 6. The materials that support you and the process as the proposal progresses are described here. They include information on the proposal process itself, materials supporting the design team in developing portions of the proposal to specifications, and materials for instructing reviewers and collecting review comments.

## CREATING MATERIALS ON THE PROPOSAL PROCESS

For the pre-proposal planning meeting, the kickoff meeting, and negotiations with managers described briefly in the beginning of this section and in detail in Chapter 3, you should develop materials that describe the proposal process and the systems used to track the process. These can include the following graphics:

- A step-by-step explanation of the proposal process, such as Example 4-1

- An explanation of the anti-chaos theory, as in Example 4-2

- A description of your method for working on the network, shown in Example 4-3.

### Creating Sample Themes, Discriminators, Theme Statements, and Action Captions

Chapter 7 describes in detail the process of developing win themes, discriminators, theme statements, and action captions. It also delineates features and benefits.

Contributors who are new to the proposal process sometimes need examples to support them in developing these standard proposal elements. Search your past proposals for the best examples of theme statements, action captions, and features linked with benefits to provide the team with adequate examples for developing their storyboards.

### Creating a Storyboard Format

In Chapter 8, I describe the modified storyboarding process that is common in modern companies. The storyboard format is essentially a skeleton of a final section with place holders for major pieces, such as theme statements, graphics, action captions, and primary points. Sample A of the appendices is an example.

**Example 4-1:** Sample Proposal Process Slide

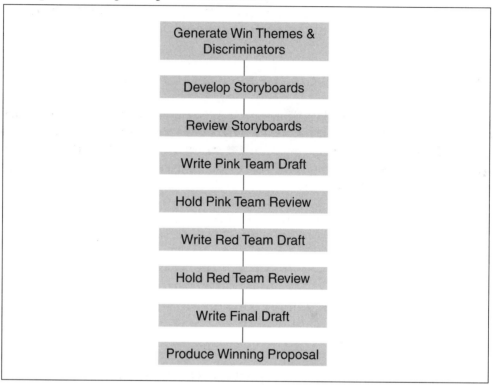

**Example 4-2:** Sample Anti-Chaos Slide

**The Anti-Chaos Theory**

- If you need something, ask for it.

- Most people are more creative in the morning; hold meetings in the morning.

- If you're working on a current contract, write for two hours on the proposal in the morning and then move on to your everyday work.

- Don't work at night unless you absolutely have to—ask yourself why if you think you do.

- If you are a consultant, let me know immediately if you feel overloaded—two consultants working seven hours are far more productive than one working 14 hours.

- Exercise, eat right, shut the proposal out during the evenings. Enjoy.

**Example 4-3:** Sample File Exchange Procedure Slide

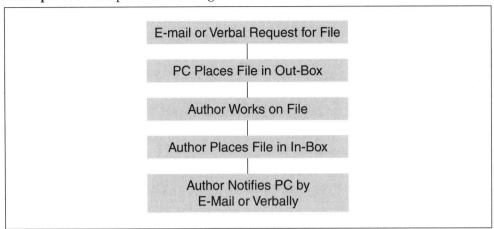

## Creating Review Support Materials

At stages in the proposal process, teams of reviewers provide comments to the proposal team. These comments are usually written on review comment sheets, review copies of the proposal, and summary slides, as described in Chapter 9.

During some reviews, the review team attempts to duplicate the formal review process that the proposal will go through once it is submitted, following evaluation criteria that are thoroughly outlined in Section M of the RFP. At other times, you can dictate how the proposal will be reviewed and the factors the review team should consider. To cover generic proposal reviews, you might develop these types of support materials:

- Guidelines for commenting regarding helpful, constructive criticism, as in Example 4-4

- Instructions for reviewing the proposal, as shown in Example 4-5

- An explanation of the rating scheme and rating process (Example 4-6)

- A review response form, as provided in Sample E.

Sample F is a second set of written instructions for distribution to reviewers before the review. These instructions incorporate guidelines for commenting.

**Example 4-4:** Sample Guidelines for Commenting

---

### Expressing Your Opinions

- Forbidden comments: "This section misses the point entirely." "They're clearly asking for. . . ." "Just answer the mail."

- Refrain from sharing negative interpretations, unless they are critical to an argument for or against a particular strategy.

- In your markup, suggest new wording without saying why.

- Own your comments by using "I think. . . ."

- Be specific and thorough. Use sentences.

- For big problems, coordinate your response with other reviewers and the entire review team.

- Identify a solution for each problem.

---

**Example 4-5:** Sample Review Instructions Slides

---

### Proposal Instructions

- Read your assigned section and mark your proposal.

- Meet with any reviewers who are reviewing the same section.

- Complete the review forms or rate the sections.

- Develop three strategies for improving deficient sections.

- Convene with the review team.

- Review your assessment with other reviewers.

- Prepare slides with other reviewers.

- Present results to the proposal team.

---

**Example 4-6:** Sample Rating Scheme and Instructions for Use

---

**The Rating Scheme**

- **Green**: This section is ready to go as is or with minor revisions.

- **Blue**: This section needs work; provide three or more solid suggestions for improvement.

- **Red**: This section needs a significant overhaul; provide three or more solid suggestions for improvement and identify resources that could be used to make the repairs.

**Rating the Proposal**

- **Compliance**: Is this section compliant with Sections C, L, and M?

- **Organizational Issues**: Is this section organized in such a way that the most important information is obvious to the reviewer?

- **Content Issues**: Is the section complete? Are the right examples used? The right graphics? Do the graphics support the text, and vice versa?

- **Stylistic Issues**: Are the theme statements and action captions complete and meaningful?

---

You simplify your life by having these things on hand. If you must modify them quickly for a particular proposal, do so on a copy of the form or graphic so that you can use the original again and again.

## Creating Proposal Team Support Materials

Some proposal coordinators provide little guidance to the proposal team in the form of boilerplate, style guides, storyboard formats, pre-defined styles, and formatted files, hoping that editors or word processors will make things right later on. I am in favor of over-supporting rather than under-supporting the proposal team. To those who claim that style guides are unread and pre-formatting is unnecessary, I say you can't read something that's not offered, and you can't support the proposal team enough.

I cover some aspects of pre-formatting files later in this section under "Setting Up a Proposal Configuration Control System," because the issues of formatting and configuration control overlap. Here I cover materials that are applicable to most of the proposals that will go through your shop. You can create these support materials and use them again and again.

### Preparing a Style Guide

Proposal coordinators who are backed by a fleet of experienced editors might not need a style guide. A competent copyeditor can transform a proposal from good to terrific with one pass, increasing the proposal coordinator's confidence enormously.

Unfortunately, copyeditors are becoming anachronisms. The advent of spelling and grammar checkers and the basic trend toward downsizing have endangered the copyeditor species, putting a greater burden for proposal perfection on the contributors and the proposal coordinator. For this reason, it is in the proposal coordinator's best interests to create a style guide.

Large corporations often have formal style guides that dictate how and where the company name will appear, who gets credit for reports and where, names of organizations within the enterprise, and similar material. You don't need an inch-thick manual; you need to demonstrate active voice, correct common mistakes, and illustrate the proper format for common terms or product names. Sample B is a sample style guide that you can steal if you want.

### Looking Forward to Production

I believe that one of the clearest differentiators among proposal coordinators (or capture managers) is the degree to which that person understands and respects the production process. People who understand it and the unfettered frustration that arises when graphics are too big to fit the page and can't be shrunk down without becoming unreadable; when illustrations come in quick succession and can't be nicely spaced to create a pleasing page; when the numbering scheme is discombobulated so that you can't understand which table goes where; will surely plan for production before the first word is on the page.

Chapter 6 will tell you how to get a head start before the design team even appears.

## Compiling Boilerplate

Unless yours is a brand new company, someone in your organization has written proposals before. Within the old proposals, you might find explanations of your management structure, compensation plan, standard methodologies, or approaches to various technical issues. All these materials are fodder for new proposals. They offer a jumping-off point for proposal contributors who can't seem to type the first word or can be full-blown treatments of certain topics that can be borrowed verbatim.

If you have electronic copies of previous proposals, copy the various sections and group them with similar materials in shared computer directories: Technical, Management, Networking, Software, Help Desk, etc. You might also keep similarly grouped hard-copy files to duplicate and distribute to the design team at the kickoff meeting. Putting paper in someone's hands is often more effective than pointing the way to a resource that contributors must seek on their own.

When you're thinking of boilerplate, include graphics and pictures. In my current area of business, we increasingly use photographs to show elements of past performance and illustrate work in progress. We also reuse a particular set of graphics in most of our proposals. We tweak the graphics here and there to make them specific to the proposal at hand, but this requires little effort when the boilerplate graphic is available. In fact, my boilerplate folder includes a host of reusable materials, such as covers and spines, logos, customer surveys, subcontracting plans, conditional employment agreements, and anything that might be reused with minor modification. Other items that we use again and again include financial statements, bank references, and contract lists. Also maintain a file containing your Dun & Bradstreet's DUNS number, standard industrial classification (SIC) codes, employee identification number (EIN or FEIN), bonding agent information, state, and type of incorporation (partnership, C corporation, S corporation, etc.).

The future of boilerplate materials—which has already arrived in some companies—is posting and sharing materials over a corporate intranet. This is a boon for those who work in distributed environments, with proposal contributors in other offices in distant states or foreign countries. An intranet allows people who work together to share resources without incurring long-distance phone and fax costs.

If you don't have an intranet in your company, suggest it to the computer support staff. Keep in mind that you'll want to post boilerplate in easily downloadable files that maintain their formats as much as possible so that the proposal team doesn't need to fool with unintended line breaks and other technical glitches.

## SETTING UP A PROPOSAL CONFIGURATION CONTROL SYSTEM

Configuration control in software and hardware parlance means a set of the methods and procedures used to document the hardware and software active in development, test, and operational environments. In proposal development, configuration control consists of methods and procedures used to make sure that no information is lost and that the most recent version of the proposal is captured in a safe location. Your configuration control system will be dependent on the hardware and software you use.

If you are not a computer whiz, you will need to get up to speed on at least the basics of computer systems to be an effective proposal coordinator. This is a not a matter of theory but one of survival. If the proposal coordinator is not personally able to manage the task of organizing and re-organizing the proposal and showing others the basics of logging on and off, backing up files, and getting to the appropriate work space, he will be dependent on computer support personnel to do so.

As with the proposal process, how you provide configuration control is not as important as the *use of configuration control*. No system works unless you use it religiously.

The goal in setting up a networked server for a proposal is providing access to all information that the writer needs while blocking access to information that the writer doesn't need. My preferred way of doing this is to create a directory or folder for the proposal using a full or abbreviated name, such as FDIC, under which I create two subdirectories: Cost and Proposal. Access to the Cost branch of this tree is blocked for all persons except the capture manager and pricing personnel. Access to the Proposal area is available to all contributors.

Under the Proposal directory, I create several more directories or folders:

- *Admin.* Admin is where I store copies of the proposal schedule and memos to the team, style guides, storyboard forms, and similar manuals.

- *Background (or Backgrd).* Background information can include a soft copy of the RFP and the proposal outline, past performance data, boilerplate, and any other information that might be valuable to the writers.

- *Active*. In this directory, I create a subdirectory for each volume of the proposal except cost.

- *In/Out*. If the proposal team is large, you can create an In/Out directory with Inbox and Outbox subdirectories. The true control freak can limit writer access to the Inbox and Outbox directories, as explained below.

- *Old*. The Old directory holds old versions of the proposal. For example, when the Pink Team draft is completed, I move it to a subdirectory called Pink under the Old directory. You can limit the access to this directory if you want.

Some systems allow more flexibility in naming directories than others, but the structure is similar in most cases. The tree structure for the active directory looks something like Example 4-7.

If you have a small proposal team, you can often allow individuals to work within the active directory with the caveat that team members must work only on the section to which they are assigned, unless they have permission from the assigned writer.

**Example 4-7:** Sample Proposal Tree Structure

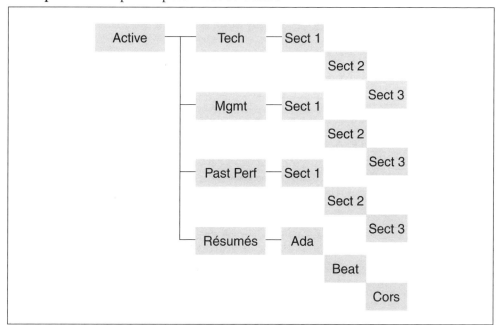

Another rule for this type of setup—and all setups, in fact—is that the writers should *never* rename a file. Renaming creates questions about the most recent version and drives all concerned crazy.

If you're working with a large proposal team, it is better to hand out and receive updated files through the Outbox and Inbox following these steps:

- Writer requests a file

- Proposal coordinator moves (or copies) the file from the Text directory to the Outbox

- Writer works on the file

- Writer returns the file to the Inbox

- Proposal coordinator moves (or copies) the file from the Inbox to the Text directory.

The Inbox/Outbox method offers sole control over what is written to the Active directory, which can be particularly helpful if team members carry the can't-follow-directions gene. For example, if a contributor has renamed the file, the proposal coordinator can correct the problem before it contaminates the system. On the other hand, this procedure takes time, which is the price you pay for preventing unintentional sabotage.

### Using Other Information-Sharing Capabilities

I've tried to avoid system-specific instructions throughout this guide. Nevertheless, various systems have capabilities that can enhance configuration control. For example, Microsoft® Word has a "Summary Info" option under the File directory that you can use to mark files that are copied out of the Active directory. You can also use various locking capabilities, color-coding schemes, or newer information-sharing software.

I suggest that you balance ease of use with safety, taking into consideration your own potential to make mistakes. If you use a color-coding system, you must rely on yourself to remember to change the color code when you copy a file from the Active directory to the Outbox. A system that automatically locks a file when it is copied to the Outbox also automatically forces configuration control. If your system provides the capability to perform such feats, through a macro or groupware mechanism, all the better.

## Maintaining the Hard-Copy File

Until our online systems are more reliable and available whenever we need them, I will keep a hard copy of all documents associated with each bid. I file a copy of the RFP and each amendment, plus correspondence, for each proposal we submit, in case I lose a copy of an amendment or need a clean cover sheet at the last minute.

## Backing Up the Proposal

Most networked systems are backed up partially each night and fully each week, at a minimum. Ask your network administrator how the system is backed up—but only as a backup for a backup. You should back up your proposal nightly to another server or to your own hard disk so that you have a full proposal if your primary server fails. At the very least, back up the Active, Inbox, and Outbox directories. Require that individuals who have checked out files back up those files nightly or deposit a copy in the Inbox so that you can back it up.

## HANDLING PROPOSAL TEAM LOGISTICS

As a consultant, I've found that the biggest impediments to productivity are poor equipment and facilities. On the other side of the coin, where support is organized and the equipment and facilities are comfortable, my job is a breeze.

In the planning session with the capture manager, you will get a general idea who will be working where. Start planning to support the people who will be working in your facility and those who will be telecommuting as follows:

- Locate and reserve space for desks, computers, telephones, and meetings.

- Provide computer passwords, telephone message passwords, and e-mail accounts.

- Provide office supplies, from pencils to tape.

- Create and distribute confidentiality agreements.

- Arrange for building and office access.

- Prepare in-house staff.

### Situating Desks, Computers, and Phones

A primary obstacle to productivity is noise, and noise in the office usually comes from other people doing what other people do—talk on the phone, chat with their neighbors, think aloud. I realize that some companies cannot afford to provide individual spaces for proposal writers; nevertheless, I advise you to do so if at all possible. Individual spaces not only provide a quiet environment for writing but also a semblance of privacy after long meetings or tense interactions.

If individual offices are not available, sound barriers are the next-best alternative, with plenty of space between desks a last-ditch choice. Workstations that face each another or are smack up against each other create a situation in which a mild case of indigestion becomes cause for roaming around the office rather than sitting down to write.

Provide a computer, phone, and at least as much space as a normal desktop for each workstation. If your computer workstations are small, leaving no room for materials to be stacked beside them, provide a table for storage. Provide the fastest computer you can afford—it will make a big difference in productivity, while reducing frustration.

A one-to-one ratio of phones to team members is ideal and also vastly improves productivity by: (1) increasing the number of times that a caller actually speaks to the party called and (2) reducing the interruptions to others in the room each time the phone rings. Anything less than a one-to-one ratio is second best and gets worse as the number of persons sharing a phone increases. Do what you can.

If possible, reserve small and large meeting spaces for blocks of time. You will need large conference rooms for storyboarding and reviews. Small rooms are adequate for meetings of two or three contributors who are coordinating their sections. If you provide small rooms, team members won't interrupt others who are too polite to ask for quiet.

### Providing Computer Access, Phone Message Access, and E-mail Accounts

Proposal contributors need computer access, phone message access, and e-mail access. Some network operating systems allow concurrent access to a directory under a single password for a limited number of people. If you have this capability, I would use it to set up initial access to appropriate directories before your proposal team arrives. Alternatively, you can collect the names of all the persons who will be working on the proposal and set up an individual account for each using a password that you assign. Plan to walk each writer through the first logon process or provide step-by-step instructions for the writer to follow.

Most phone systems require access codes to retrieve messages. Before your team arrives, set up these access codes with the system administrator, label the phones with the full number and the message retrieval code, and place a set of instructions for retrieving messages under the phone. To make this easy, label each workstation with a code, such as Work1, and use the same name as the access code for the accompanying phone and even the network password for the computer, as shown in Example 4-8.

**Example 4-8:** Sample Password Setups

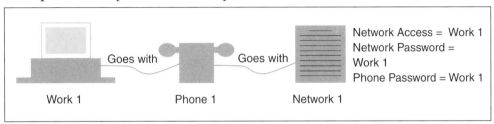

Setting up e-mail access is trickier because you will want to use the company's standard convention for naming e-mail accounts for the visiting proposal team. If you use a standard convention, such as first initial and last name, individuals who are not direct members of the proposal team but who are exchanging information with the team can guess at the e-mail address to which they can send a message.

To set up e-mail accounts before the team arrives, you'll need at least the first initial and last name of each member. If you ask for this information at the pre-proposal planning meeting (Chapter 7), you should receive it one jump ahead of design team invasion.

### Providing Accessories

The proposal team will need all the typical office accessories during its stay in your office:

- Tablets

- Pencils

- Pens

- Phone message pads

- Colored flags to mark RFP sections

- Adhesive notes to write remarks on the RFP

- Three-hole punch to put printouts into binders

- Stapler

- Scotch tape

- Ruler

- Scissors

- Markers for white boards.

If your supply cabinet is perpetually locked, place the items listed above in an unlocked area so the proposal team can use them freely. Of course, remind the team to return common supplies to the designated area after use.


**Distributing Confidentiality Agreements**

For your own protection, ask team employees to sign confidentiality agreements before they arrive at your office. Send these to the point persons for your teammates and make sure that all are signed and returned before the kickoff meeting.


**Arranging for Building and Office Access**

I am totally opposed to working evening and weekends and therefore think it's unnecessary to provide cards or access codes for weekend and evening work. Do so if you must. Then ask why you must—again and again. Also make sure you know the codes of cipher locks or the hiding places for keys.

**Preparing In-house Staff**

If consultants will be extracting information from in-house staff, the proposal coordinator should prepare the internal staff for the upcoming demands. In many recent proposals, for example, the government asked offerors to provide home phone numbers on the résumés of proposed personnel. This requirement was most easily handled through the human resources department, which maintains employee numbers on file, rather than from each individual. A quick call in advance speeds the process while ensuring the team member that the consultant isn't a visiting alien from Mars.

These steps will eventually pay off big time. In the organization where I now work, it has taken a mix of cajoling, begging, and screaming to get what I want for the people who are working with me. Now, however, the folks I deal with regularly in the information technology department, on the secretarial staff, and among the professional employees respond quickly and understand why they do so. That feels good.

# CHAPTER 5

# Tracking the RFP

A funny thing happened on the way to the future: The Internet, while saving time and money in accomplishing day-to-day functions in almost any other aspect of our lives, has created more work for the proposal manager.

Why is this? In pre-Internet days, when most communication was handled through the U.S. Postal Service, the government took responsibility for sending all announcements, solicitations, and amendments to contractors through the mail. Moreover, once a piece of mail was sent, a government representative associated with a particular solicitation often followed up with the contractor to make sure the mail arrived at the correct destination. An incorrectly typed label could, after all, be reason for a charge of unfairness or even a full-blown protest. The government, therefore, tended to be meticulous in ensuring that each company on the bidders list had all applicable documents in hand.

With the advent of the Internet, the government has placed the burden of obtaining copies of procurement documents firmly in the hands of the contractor. This is indeed a boon to us as taxpayers at the same time that it is a bust to us as proposal coordinators. As a consequence of the Internet, contractors who bid aggressively across agency boundaries must track solicitations on a hodgepodge of Internet sites, each with its own process and some with barely a process at all.

Once you successfully track the release of solicitations you want to bid, you are then responsible for downloading associated procurement documents. Not always knowing whether or not amendments will be forthcoming, you are then responsible for re-checking each site until the date the proposal is submitted to ensure that no amendment has been released or to download the amendment if one has been.

In a modestly sized business, tracking and downloading can be a part-time job, made more frustrating by not-ready-for-prime-time software glitches. I have downloaded thousands of unnumbered pages that cannot be reassembled once a copier error has occurred. And assistant after assistant in my office has complained about enormous PDF files that lock up and crash their computers. We have been unable to download a few files associated with solicitations because of their size and our limited computer capacity. When I notified the government of the problem I got a response that amounts to "tough luck."

More horrific, I have actually missed the posting of an important solicitation because I was already working on a proposal that demanded my full-time attention. I think I can safely say that we lost that bid because we were late off the starting line and, with our resources devoted elsewhere, couldn't make up the lost time.

But enough whining. I offer several rules for this stage of the Internet age:

- Take advantage of free or commercial services available to help you, even if you must wade through advertising to use them.

- Develop a tracking spreadsheet or database to assist in prospecting.

- Establish a schedule for visiting Internet sites, and stick to it. You will need to visit each site at least once a week or more often if you're in the middle of the proposal process. You cannot afford to miss a solicitation update.

- Upgrade any computers involved with downloading files to at least 128 K memory.

- Give the government feedback about the processes that various agencies are establishing as—or before—they are established.

## GOVERNMENT INTERNET SERVICES

My primary sites for tracking solicitations are cbdnet.gpo.gov and www.fedbizopps.gov. Cbdnet.gpo.gov, as the name suggests, is the online version of the *Commerce Business Daily* and is available free to anyone with Internet access.

Www.fedbizopps.gov is a project of the General Services Administration, the National Aeronautics and Space Administration, the Department of Transportation, and a growing number of other government agencies. Www.fedbizopps.gov goes beyond the online CBD in being a repository for all information associated with a particular solicitation.

Because I have found it difficult to conceptualize these sites in their proper context, initially causing some problems in developing a tracking strategy, I will explain them more explicitly. As I discussed in Chapter 1, under the Federal Acquisition Regulation (the FAR) the government is required to announce to the public all procurements that exceed a certain dollar threshold. The printed *Commerce Business Daily* is the medium for those announcements, and it remains the definitive source, although the online CBD is available.

The mission of the CBD is merely to notify contractors that a solicitation is available or will become available at some time in the future. Normally, the CBD will provide the contractor with instructions on where the contractor can follow up with the solicitation. In the "good old days," this was almost certainly a phone number or address that the contractor could call or write to be placed on the bidders list. Thereafter, the individual agency took over the process and was responsible for sending solicitation documents to the contractors. In today's environment, the follow-up instructions normally point the contractor to a website where the full solicitation and any forthcoming amendments will be posted at a specified or unspecified date.

This is where www.fedbizopps.gov comes in. Www.fedbizopps.gov has taken the online process one step further by creating a repository for all announcements and documents associated with a particular solicitation. If a solicitation is listed here, the contractor can register to receive e-mail notices when the solicitation is released and any time thereafter when amendments or other addenda are posted. When the contractor receives the e-mail notification, it is then the contractor's responsibility to go to the website and download the documents.

You should also know, however, that while some branches of the government have taken on the task of notifying contractors about updates to solicitations posted on the website, the government does not guarantee that the notification will work. It remains the contractor's responsibility to keep abreast of solicitations and download documents.

This "buyer beware" caveat is particularly important for folks with sketchy e-mail service. Although it is my experience that the www.fedbizopps.gov site is faithful in its e-mail notifications, I have also experienced occasions when I don't receive e-mails that are sent through a variety of e-mail providers. That is, the government sends, but I don't receive. Until e-mail is fail-safe, there is no way of knowing if you've missed an update without regularly visiting the site. *PROBABLY FIXED AS OF 2008*

Www.fedbizopps.gov is nevertheless the best of Internet solicitation posting sites at this time. It is light years ahead of agencies that don't provide any notification of new postings, that post solicitation documents on a variety of sites strewn across the Internet, or that issue an announcement and then drag their feet in posting the solicitation. I have, for example, experienced instances in which a solicitation was announced in May and was not released until October. In the meantime, it was my responsibility to check the website at least weekly to see if the solicitation was posted. Phone calls to the contracting specialist went unanswered.

## COMMERCIAL INTERNET SERVICES

The online CBD, like the written version, is organized with similar products and services under an alphanumeric coding system, making it easier for government and commercial companies to send bulk notices to contractors through e-mail. Consequently, several companies have jumped into the Internet fray to simplify the bid tracking process for profit.

I use www.govcon.com and www.bidnet.com, the former to receive bid notices from CBD and the latter to receive notices from state and local governments. Www.govcon.com, which is currently free, grabs information from the online CBD and sends it by CBD category to a subscriber's e-mail address. Www.bidnet.com, which charges for its services, groups bid notices by standard industrial codes (SIC codes) and by state and also e-mails them to contractors.

I'm sure that as the Internet evolves, similar services will be available, either for free or fee, and that you will have the same problem that we have keeping up with what's new and better. We've almost arrived at the conclusion that we need a full-time person to do our Internet tracking, so I've been thinking about what that person will do, as you'll read below.

## STAFFING THE TRACKING FUNCTION

Now that the burden of tracking solicitations has been shifted to the contractor, it is particularly important for you to stay abreast of changes in sites, new procurement sites, and services that will make your job easier.

You'll probably want to use a combination of automated and human resources in your process, as we do. Our current process for tracking bids goes something like this:

- We receive a bid notice from one of the e-mail services described above. The notice is an abbreviated version of the full announcement, which can be an announcement of a future posting, solicitation release, or amendment. The announcement can also be something tangential, such as a notice that a solicitation that was originally announced as a full and open competition will now be set aside for small and minority-owned businesses.

- Within the announcement is a web address. If the notice looks promising or is associated with a solicitation that is already in progress, I click on the hyperlink to that address.

- I read the whole of the announcement and decide whether or not it is in our general area of interest. If it is, I print the address and pass it along to my manager, who makes the ultimate decision whether or not we will continue to track the bid.

- If we decide to track the bid, I keep the bid notice in a book and enter salient features of the bid into a spreadsheet, discussed below.

- I also follow the instructions in the announcement for signing up for the bidders list. This might mean faxing a letter to the contracting officer, calling the contracting officer, or registering online to receive solicitation and amendment announcements.

- Each day I flip through the book of notices, paying more attention to the solicitations that are imminent and less to those that are still in the distant future.

- When RFPs or amendments are released, I download them.

This job has now outgrown me. In our fairly small government contracting division, we are fast approaching the time when we need a full-time person just to track RFPs, download them, pass them on to persons who can confirm that we want to bid on the jobs, and move on to the next website. That person must have the following capabilities:

- *Ease with the Internet and associated software skills.* You've read my rantings about too-big files and jumbled page numbers. This job is not for the easily confused. Online files are sometimes compressed and must be uncompressed once downloaded. Other files are enormous, and still others can't be printed once they are downloaded because of page size or software origin.

The person who tracks and downloads the RFPs must have the ability to diagnose and overcome technical problems, articulate those problems, and seek help from the Webmaster or contracting officer, where required.

- *Ability to make gross judgments about issues such as the substance of the procurement, its dollar size, and location with respect to your company's areas of business.* The person who tracks the solicitation doesn't need to make final decisions, but he should be able to separate the wheat from the chaff in a general way.

    Alternatively, the tracker can receive all the bid notices within a certain category, print them, and pass them along to the person who makes the ultimate decision.

- *Ability to communicate with the government for hard-copy RFPs.* At the same time that most RFPs are posted on the Internet, some are still distributed in hard copy. You'll want to have a single process for RFPs, online or not, so you'll want the RFP tracker to be able to communicate with the government through faxes, e-mail, or the U.S. mail.

The point here is that you want all RFPs to arrive at your organization through the same portal and move through the same process, regardless of whether they are Internet-based or mailed. This has always been the case—even when all RFPs were mailed—but it has become even more important now that the Internet has confused the tracking process. The RFP tracker should be reliable and the process expeditious. It can't involve people who are too busy to look at newly arrived RFPs or to cull through RFP announcements, because you'll get behind before you even get started.

If the RFP tracker is not a great writer but is a reliable conduit, create a standard letter or e-mail that person can send to the contracting officer to place your company's name on the bidders list. Use the tracker's name in the address so that the RFP is sent directly to him.

The RFP tracker should allocate a certain portion of the day to tracking the bids and updating your tracking documentation without major interruption. Internet postings are highly confusing. The variation in form and content, in etiquette, and in basic tenets of fair play as expressed on government Internet sites are extreme. For example, I literally forgot for quite a while that the government is not obligated to announce the release of an RFP in the printed CBD or the Internet equivalent because I'd semi-unconsciously begun to see www.fedbizopps.gov, which *does* announce RFP and amendment postings, as the standard for Internet solicitations. In fact, www.fedbizopps.gov is the exception, rather than the standard, even as a growing number of agencies are joining its ranks.

But you really have to experience this to understand what I'm fuming about, to conceptualize the job of the RFP tracker, and to empathize with the pitfalls inherent with the responsibility. This is why it's important for the proposal coordinator to control the RFP tracking position actively and to assist in formulating emerging processes as they evolve inside and outside your company.

### Keeping Abreast of New Sites and Features

Another function that could be added to the tracker's responsibilities is that of staying abreast of new sites and new features on old sites. Every so often—perhaps quarterly—someone from your organization should see what's out there. Using a variety of search engines, search on terms like "government," "contracting," or "procurement," and see what turns up. If the search is productive, the tracker can print out the listing and work her way through the sites to see what each has to offer.

### Developing a Tracking Spreadsheet or Database

At any given time, it is not unusual to be tracking ten or more solicitations, each on a different timeline and website. This can be tedious and confusing, so it is best to develop a database or spreadsheet that works as a tickler file. While there are many products for tracking sales in the commercial arena, I am unaware of any that is specifically tailored to the government contracting arena. I wouldn't rule it out, however, so you may want to search the Internet for products. My preferred product would contain at least the following fields:

- Agency

- Solicitation number

- Procurement name

- Procurement description

- Procurement website

- Projected release date

- Projected due date

- Contracting officer

- Contracting officer phone number

- Log of contacts.

The idea is to snatch pertinent information from the CBD and compile it in a database that is specific to your company. Then you record information each time you check on a website or call a contracting officer so that you have an ongoing reminder of the status of the procurement. Sort the procurements in the order of the release dates, with those that are in the proposal process or close to release on top and those that are further out on the bottom.

If you go use a network to connect to the Internet, you can create a hyperlink in the web field that takes you from the spreadsheet or database directly to the Internet site with a single click.

If several individuals track RFPs, you might also want to use software that allows those people to share database access at one time.

### Upgrading Your Computer RAM

Internet postings place demands on your computer's memory. If RFPs in your industry typically include items such as inventory printouts or any sort or graphics that would be software-dependent, they'll probably be loaded into PDF files, which grow very big very quickly. I have found that computers with less than 126 megabytes of random access memory (RAM) cannot handle these files. Upgrade your computer to downgrade your stress.

## PROVIDING FEEDBACK TO THE GOVERNMENT

Internet procurement sites are evolving and will continue to change quickly as the underlying technologies change. Even as this document goes to press, for example, www.cbdnet.gov is offering expanded e-mail services.

Take an active role in creating the kind of websites that work for the government and contractors by offering feedback—even if the agencies you deal with don't ask for it.

Don't just complain to the contracting representative handling a particular solicitation. Rather, put your ideas in writing and send them to the highest procurement official in the agency. Be specific and, wherever possible, emphasize the need for a fair, unimpeachable process that will protect the agency from protests. My advice to the government would include the following ideas, which you are welcome to use in your letters:

- *Develop a central procurement location for all federal procurements.* This is a big undertaking, but it will be worth it. The logical starting point for this website is some combination of the two sites I mentioned, cbdnet.gpo.gov and www.fedbizopps.gov.

- *Set a cut-off point for issuing paper or CD ROM solicitations.* If the Internet is the standard, make it the standard. Get rid of other types of solicitations to eliminate confusion.

- *Make e-mail notification mandatory.* Some Internet sites offer no e-mail announcements of solicitation releases or updates. This places an enormous burden on the contractor and fully eliminates any burden on the government. E-mail notifications should be mandatory.

- *Set timelines between announcement and release.* Announcing that an RFP will be released and then postponing that release indefinitely without notifying the bidders is just institutionalized rudeness. The Internet offers an opportunity to communicate with hundreds of companies without leaving a desk. The government should use it. All they need to do is post a notice saying, "This solicitation has been delayed for three (or five, or ten) months."

- *Number every page of a solicitation, including attachments.* Government representatives who answer contractor questions or issue amendments should understand the implications of page numbering in locating a particular sentence, clause, or paragraph. There is no substitute for page numbers, and that should be evident.

- *Avoid scanned documents.* Every little smudge on a scanned page takes up some memory in your computer, so that even very small documents can turn into memory hogs. There is no reason to put up with this. Whatever your personal feelings about Microsoft® may be, MS Word is now the tacit industry standard for word processing, and documents should be converted to that format whenever possible. If graphics or maps must be scanned, provide instructions for printing.

- *Forbid amendments without change bars.* This is only the Internet reincarnation of an old problem. No contractor should be required to re-read a solicitation line by line, comparing it to an earlier version, to figure out where changes have been made. This is why change bars were conceived. They should be mandatory for amendments.

Again, the ultimate goal should be a fair procurement executed in good faith.

## SENDING FREEDOM OF INFORMATION ACT REQUESTS

Internet tracking of the RFP places the proposal coordinator on the front end of the proposal process and may make her the logical point of control for the Freedom of Information Act request—if it makes sense to use one.

As I mentioned earlier, the Freedom of Information Act, known as FOIA, allows the public to request of the government certain types of unclassified information. This includes copies of current contracts for products and services. For some repetitive types of contracts, a copy of the current contract is the jumping-off point for pricing a new bid. Some people use the requested contract to make a final bid or no bid decision. Certain types of businesses submit FOIA requests as a routine part of the proposal process.

Create a standard FOIA letter and send it to the FOIA officer at the target agency as soon as the CBD announcement of an imminent proposal is made. The letter need not be any fancier than the one shown in Example 5-1.

**Example 5-1:** Sample FOIA Letter

---

January 4, 2001

Ms. Jane Doe
FOIA Officer
General Services Administration
234 General Drive, Suite 10
Philadelphia, PA 17452

RFP:  23-675792-00
        Administrative Services, Philadelphia Region

Dear Ms. Doe:

This is a request under the Freedom of Information Act regarding the above-named solicitation. Please provide us with copies of the current contract, including all clauses with any changes and modifications.

We are prepared to pay up to $200.00 in servicing and copying costs for fulfillment of this request. Please call me at (717) 352-0927 if you expect costs to exceed that amount.

Sincerely,

Proposal Coordinator

---

Don't wait until the RFP is released, or you may receive the FOIA response after the proposal is due. Also be aware that some contracting officers include the current contract in the bidders library to avoid responding to individual FOIA requests. Other officers have been known to deny requests on the grounds that the contract contains proprietary information. Still other organizations post current contracts on the Internet, where they are available to all.

Familiarize yourself with the FOIA legislation so that you can argue in your company's defense if you disagree with the FOIA decision. I would also tend to argue any FOIA points only with the FOIA officer, not with the contracting officer, so that you know you're dealing with someone whose primary job is to interpret the law.

*Use of "strawman" proposal when a customized solution is required.*

## MAKING THE BID/NO BID DECISION

Some companies make informal bid or no bid decisions among senior managers and pricing personnel after taking a quick look at a draft RFP or current contract and making a ballpark assessment of its size and potential profitability. Others—particularly those specializing in products and services that are tailored to a specific customer's needs—may go beyond the ballpark to create a "strawman" solution, estimate the cost of that solution, and evaluate the solution in comparison to competitors' solutions. The formal procedure can include detailed, weighted competitive analyses, with a final score for each expected participant in the bid.

*R&D CONTRACTS*

As noted above, the FOIA can be used in the bid/no bid decision. If your FOIA request is successful—and they usually are if the contract is a repetitive support contract that doesn't involve proprietary secrets—it is one piece of information to be assessed with others in deciding whether or not a particular contract is an appropriate target for your company.

The resources available to produce the proposal may also be factored into the bid decision. If your staff is already gainfully employed producing another proposal with a good chance of winning, your company may choose not to bid on a longshot. On the other hand, if your organization is already involved in producing another proposal and an equally important opportunity with an equal potential for success comes along, you may want to bring in temporary resources to produce the proposals in tandem. *pp-179-183*

The bid/no bid meeting is an absolute necessity for large companies bidding large jobs because the investment in the proposal and tangential activities, such as prototype development, benchmarking, or live test demonstrations, can run into millions of dollars. It makes no sense to spend this amount of money if a competitor's product or service is a sure winner.

A disciplined bid/no bid meeting is also an important milestone in a successful proposal process for small and mid-sized bids because it begins the process of analyzing competitors, conceptualizing the solution, and setting the pricing strategy. All these activities might happen independently without a meeting, but the discipline of the meeting sets the tone for the rest of the proposal process.

The proposal coordinator's role is to make sure the meeting happens and to shepherd the other players through their responsibilities. Typically, the capture manager creates a competitive analysis for the bid/no bid meeting that can later be modified for the kickoff meeting if the company chooses to move ahead with the bid (see Example 5-2). Note that the information in the competitive analysis also underlies the themes and discriminators that are developed later in the proposal process.

The pricing specialist or the capture manager creates a similar analysis focusing on where competitors would be priced in relation to each another. Both of these analyses are based on a combination of best guesses and research, including FOIA data, public pricing information for off-the-shelf products, wage determinations and union agreements, in-house salaries and industry association surveys, and similar information.

**Example 5-2:** Sample Competitive Analysis

| Competitor | Characteristics of Bid/Company | Pros | Cons | Win Potential |
|---|---|---|---|---|
| ABC Company | ABC minicomputers are the heart of the proposed system | Priced right | Unreliable system | Medium |
| | Huge corporation | Unending resources | Lack of accountability at upper levels | |
| EFG Wireless | Upgrade of the system currently in use | The agency knows the system | Outdated interface | Medium |
| | Strong team with unusually tough-to-beat wireless capability | Incumbent | Poor service reputation | |

| Tricon Support | Distributed system with Loren backbone | Aggressive marketing campaign as innovative engineering leader | New, relatively unproven technology | High |
|---|---|---|---|---|
| | Teamed with Loren | Partnership offers strong user support | None | |

The proposal coordinator might be asked to prepare a budget for the proposal, including the cost of supplementary resources, such as temporary writers, editors, or production staff. The budget can be prepared from a per-page estimate, based on the page requirements of previous proposals for similar services or from an estimate of hours required for the effort multiplied by the loaded hourly rates for participating individuals. The per-page estimate, described also in Chapter 3, is an average cost per page derived from a long-term analysis of the cost of proposals in your organization. Either method can, but does not need to, include the cost of design team's time.

Your contribution might look like Example 5-3.

The result of the bid/no bid meeting is a definitive decision to move ahead or drop the bid. A side benefit is a better understanding of your competitors and a greater awareness of the resources used in the proposal process and the real costs associated with them—something that many people rarely or never see.

**Example 5-3:** Estimated Proposal Costs

| Position | Hours | Loaded Hourly Rate | Total |
|---|---|---|---|
| Proposal Coordinator | 80 | $45 | $3,600 |
| Temporary Writers | 160 x 2 | $70 | $22,400 |
| Production Manager | 10 | $35 | $350 |
| Graphics | 40 | $30 | $1,200 |
| Desktop Publishing | 40 | $25 | $1,000 |
| Total | | | $28,550 |

If you've decided to drop a bid as a prime contractor, you might still investigate the possibility of subcontracting. You can apply any of the analyses that you use for a prime contract to assess the feasibility of a subcontract.

## CHAPTER 6

# *Preparing for Production*

Thinking about production of the proposal before you begin to create one, or even before you create a proposal shop, is an absolute necessity. Once the proposal goes into production, the schedule is blocked in. The deadline must be met; failure is not a possibility. A difficult production process leads to staff frustration and sleepless nights—precisely what we're trying to avoid.

The proposal coordinator also has a vested interest in the overall look of the proposal, which can be influenced by the hardware and software used, the quality of the production staff, and even the quality of the copier. With this in mind, the proposal coordinator must be concerned with how the proposal is produced, whether or not he manages production.

## THINKING ABOUT HARDWARE AND SOFTWARE

I can't make your choice of hardware or software for you, but I've got some opinions that you can weigh when making your choices:

- Macintoshes are clearly superior for almost any type of production task, but they're impractical to use if you're dealing with government agencies that require soft-copy formats submitted in PC-compatible files with the hard-copy proposals—although some have done it.

- Desktop publishing products such as QuarkXPress™ or Adobe® PageMaker® are far better at handling graphics and pictures than word processing software, but they have some serious drawbacks as well. PageMaker® has a barely adequate capability for creating tables, for example, and moving tables from Microsoft® Word to PageMaker® is not the copy-and-paste function that it should be. Desktop publishing programs also win hands-down for producing in a two-column format or changing the format from one page to the next.

- Word processing software like Word and WordPerfect® have larger user populations and thus plenty of operators available. Either is fine for creating tables, but neither handles pictures and graphics well. On the other hand, it is easy to insert landscape-oriented pages in an otherwise portrait-oriented document using a word processing program.

- Adobe® Photoshop® or a similar program is almost mandatory for producing proposals as photographs become more popular. You'll want the capability to lighten, darken, or save pictures in various formats.

- High-end graphics programs like Adobe® Illustrator® or Macromedia® Freehand® are generally overkill for proposals, except for creating snazzy covers and spines. Corel DRAW®, Microsoft® Visio®, Claris MacDraw®, or similar programs are adequate for most purposes.

- If you generally create the same types of graphics in your proposals— a detailed phase-in plan, for example—you might want to invest in software that generates the graphic for you using activities and dates.

- Clip art or stock pictures can be an asset to your proposal if they are used sparingly.

In my mind, there is no perfect platform or perfect software available for producing proposals, so it's particularly important to stay abreast of changes in production software.

## CONTEMPLATING PRODUCTION STAFF

If you have a good production staff, you can rely on them to keep up with the newest in production software. Good production staff need to know more about software these days because of the variety of graphic and photo formats available and the possibility of incompatibility issues arising during production.

If you influence the hiring of production staff, look for desktop publishing or graphics talent and an interest in and understanding of the newest software formats. As the Internet increasingly becomes a means of sharing information throughout the organization, you'll need staff who understand how to convert from one format to another, who perhaps dabble in Internet coding languages like HTML or Java, and who don't balk at compatibility challenges.

## CREATING A FORMAT GUIDE

You also want the people who won't have anything to do with production to know what you're aiming for, so that they can help you move toward your goal rather than work against it. One way to do this is to develop a format guide that will advance your proposal toward production. There are two primary purposes for the guide:

1. In today's automated environment, proposal design team members are often the only ones to touch the soft-copy files from the storyboard phase through the Red Team review. Although you don't want writers to pay so much attention to the format that they neglect the content, you also don't want the format to be so horrendous that it becomes the focus of the reviewers' time during Pink and Red Team reviews. A format guide provides broad direction so that contributors can deal easily with format while concentrating on content.

2. Proposal graphics are a unique species of technical illustration, particularly in page-limited or two-column formats. Proposal contributors will have a better sense of what they can and cannot do if they have a concrete example of how the graphics will be sized and what their options are. Read more about this under the heading "Creating Proposal Graphics," below.

In one or two pages, the format guide illustrates the styles that have been created to ease formatting and links these styles to pre-defined formats described below. Sample E is a page layout linked to soft-copy formats.

### Preparing a Soft-copy Format

Soft-copy format files are pre-formatted files that you create to distribute to the design team. For each proposal, these files are tailored to meet the Section L formatting requirements with respect to proposal margins, line spacing, and font use. *"TEMPLATES"*

A basic template for these files can be created in advance in word processing software and maintained with your boilerplate. Even if you will be moving your proposal from a word-processing program to a desktop publishing program, the formats developed in word processing software will usually convey.

Predefined formats are sometimes called *styles*. You will want to include definitions for the following characteristics in the styles you develop:

- *Font.* The font that the government most frequently specifies in an RFP is Times or Times New Roman. In the absence of a specific requirement, you would do well to use a serif font, such as the Times family. Research has repeatedly shown that serif fonts (those with fine lines projecting from the main strokes of a character) are easier to read than sans serif fonts (those without fine lines, such as Helvetica). Use sans serif fonts only for section headings, figure labels, or tables.

- *Font styles.* Specify bold, italic, or any other appropriate style.

- *Font size.* The government most often requests that proposal type be set at 12 points. Pre-formatting at this size is your best bet.

- *Line spacing.* In many cases, the government specifies that the proposals should be single-spaced, so you should pre-define a single-spaced format. You can change the format later if the government specifies another line spacing or if you want to be adventurous. I use 1.5 spacing between lines when permitted, because it's easy on the eye.

- *Paragraph spacing.* Sometimes spaces between paragraphs make for a nicer-looking page, but they are a no-no if your proposal length is limited. Plan to allow space between paragraphs and remove it for page-limited proposals.

- *Columns.* A two-column format has advantages. First, two-column pages hold slightly more text than single-column pages—handy for page-limited proposals. A standard two-column format can have downsides as well, particularly when used in conjunction with inexperienced software users, poor word-processing programs, or computers with limited memory. Consider these things when pre-defining your proposal format. I think a single-column format is the better overall choice.

- *Justification.* Proposal text is aligned to the left or fully justified. Old research on formatting suggests that left-aligned text is easier to read than justified text if justifying causes the words to separate, creating uneven spacing within a line. Use left alignment as your standard if your word-processing or desktop publishing program does a poor job of spacing the text.

- *Indentations.* Set indentations for bullets and unnumbered subsections.

- *Place holders.* Create place holders for any pieces of the proposal that will be dropped into place at a later date. Place holders can be boxes, lines, or objects that will later be associated with graphic tracking numbers, as discussed later in this chapter. They don't need to be accurately sized, because the proposal will be evolving up to the point of final production. Example 6-1 is a sample place holder for a graphic.

**Example 6-1:** Sample Graphic Place Holder with Graphic Tracking Number

NAT00071

- *Table of contents or list of figures and tables.* If you will be using an automated capability to create a table of contents or list of figures and tables, build these into your pre-defined formats.

Any of these formatting features can be used to create pre-defined formats for the following items, at a minimum:

- Section headings to the four-digit level or lower

- Theme statements

- Figure/table titles and action captions

- Requirements, if they will appear in the proposal narrative

- Proposal narrative

- Bullets

- Unnumbered subsections

- Figure place holders

- Table place holders, if tables will be created in a graphics program

- Headers and footers.

Add to this list any other standard component of your proposals. My favored proposal format includes headers and footers. The header contains the company name on the left and the RFP number or title on the right. The footer contains a page number on the right and the non-disclosure statement on the left. I include a rule below the header text and above the footer text. Some companies insert a logo in the header.

The non-disclosure statement in the footer is a shortened version of a full non-disclosure statement placed on the cover page of the proposal, such as "Use or disclosure of information on this page is subject to the agreement on the cover page of the proposal." Sometimes the statement is specified in the RFP.

Name these standard formats so that their purpose is self-evident, as in Example 6-2.

**Example 6-2:** Sample Names for Pre-defined Formats

| Item | Pre-Format Name (Style) |
|---|---|
| Section headings to the four-digit level or lower | Heading 1<br>Heading 2<br>Heading 3<br>Heading 4 |
| Theme statements | Themes |
| Figure/table titles and action captions | Titles |
| Requirements, if they will appear in the proposal narrative | Requirements |
| Proposal narrative | Body |
| Bullets | Bullets |
| Unnumbered subsections | Subsections |
| Figure place holders | Place holder |
| Table place holders, if tables will be created in a graphics program | Place holder |
| Headers and footers | Header<br>Footer |

## Preparing Formatted Files

When contributors are ready to prepare the first version of the proposal, the proposal coordinator distributes the pre-formatted files, tailored to this particular proposal, either on the networked server, on diskettes, or using e-mail, following these steps:

1. *Create a source file.* Create one file with all the pre-defined paragraph styles and page formatting. You can use the template capability if your software provides it, with the caveat that templates are tricky and some people don't know how to use them. (Note that "template" is used here as it is used in MS Word, not as a generic term.) Your job is to develop a winning proposal, not to improve contributors' software skills. If two minutes of training will suffice, go for it. If not, follow the path of least resistance.

2. *Copy the proposal outline to the source file.* Copy the entire proposal outline into the source file.

3. *Format the proposal outline.* Use the pre-defined styles to format the proposal outline.

4. *Paste specifications.* Paste specifications from the soft copy of the RFP (or the compliance matrix, if appropriate) into the related sections of the outline.

5. *Create place holders.* Using the styles you defined, create a place holder for a theme statement, a graphic, and a graphic title. Copy this set of place holders under each major heading to at least the three-digit level. Format these place holders using the pre-defined formats.

6. *Save the source file.* Save the source file as *Source*, using any filename extensions required by your software.

7. *Create section files.* Create the individual files that will be distributed to proposal contributors by using the *Save As* feature available with most word-processing packages, duplicating the file, or copying your file to a new file with a new name. Keep the source file in case you make a mistake during step 8 or 9.

8. *Name files.* Name the files by section numbers. Your goal in naming files is to indicate the beginning and ending sections contained in the file, which can be a challenge when confronted with certain file-naming limitations. For example, the filename 131_1318 could indicate that the file contains sections 1.3.1 through 1.3.1.8, or it could mean the file contains sections 1.3.1 through 1.3.18. Do your best. When your files are numbered correctly, they should stack up sequentially in the online file directory.

9. *Delete extraneous material.* Delete all material in each file except for that material related specifically to the named sections. If you make a mistake, copy material from the source file into your section file.

The resulting files will put you far ahead of the game and will make you look terribly organized. Sample C is an example printout from a pre-formatted file—what I call a modified storyboard. The process above creates files that will look similar to those in the Sample C but contain your standard format.

Place these files on a networked server, and you're ready to go.

### Creating Standard Formats for Front Matter

Word processors or desktop publishers will eventually need a format to follow when creating the front matter for your proposal. Create a sample inside cover page, table of contents, list of figures and tables, acronym list, and cover page for appendices or addenda. Place a non-disclosure statement like the one in Example 6-3 on the inside cover page. If you don't have one, ask your corporate lawyer to write one or find a copy of any old proposal and use the statement from that proposal.

**Example 6-3:** Sample Non-disclosure Statement

> This proposal or quotation contains data that shall not be disclosed outside the Government and shall not be duplicated, used, or disclosed, in whole or in part, for any purpose other than to evaluate this proposal or quotation. If, however, a contract is awarded to this offeror or quoter as a result of, or in connection with, the submission of this data, the Government shall have the right to duplicate, use, or disclose the data to the extent provided in the resulting contract. This restriction does not limit the Government's right to use information contained in this data if it is obtained from another source without restriction. The data subject to this restriction are contained in pages as noted.

Example 6-4 is a sample inside cover page, the first page you see when you open a proposal binder.

**Example 6-4:** Sample Inside Cover Page

Computer Information
Systems Upgrade

**Volume I—Technical Proposal**

To:
Office of Information Management
New York City
1490 Broadway
New York, New York 11201

From:
Shannon Associates, Inc.
1650 Irving Street, N.W.
Washington, D.C. 20010

March 11, 2000

## CREATING PROPOSAL GRAPHICS

Graphics—both tables and figures—complement the proposal narrative. They serve several purposes, including: (1) being a touchstone for reviewers who are more visually than verbally oriented, (2) being used to present statistics that would be lost in the text, and (3) providing visual relief to the reader's eye. These are all important jobs.

Proposal graphics are an unusual species among technical illustrations, particularly when the proposal is page-limited or when the government specifies the size of the font that can be used in the graphics. When the proposal is page-limited, the graphics must be as small as possible while retaining their meaning. When the government specifies a font size for graphics, the artist must design the graphic to work around the font-size requirements while conserving space.

### Creating Figures

Many proposal consultants advise proposal developers to strive for simplicity and clarity in their proposal figures. I agree with these goals *and* think that simplicity is often a luxury that is unaffordable, particularly in page-limited proposals. Often we are forced to draft complex graphics because they describe complex processes. Clarity is all the more important.

Another goal is presenting graphics that can stand alone without accompanying narrative. Again, I think this is an admirable goal that is rarely achieved, and I'm not offended by text that explains or supports a figure.

Sizing figures is one of the more challenging aspects of creating them. In page-limited proposals, tables must also be tightly sized to prevent wasted space. The idea is to fill the space available while allowing some room—white space—to create a pleasing layout, as in Example 6-5. Too much white space, created by a figure that is poorly proportioned, makes for an awkward layout, as in Example 6-6.

For this reason the author specifies the figure's size when submitting a hand-drawn draft. The artist can then design the graphic to fit the designated space. The graphic form I've provided in Sample D requests sizing information.

**Example 6-5:** Sample Properly Sized Figure

Sizing figures is one of the more challenging parts of creating them. In page-limited proposals, tables must also be tightly sized to prevent wasted space. The idea is to fill the space available while allowing some room—white space—to create a pleasing layout, as in Example 15-1. Too much white space, created by a figure that is poorly proportioned, makes for an awkward layout, as in Example 15-2.

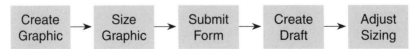

**Figure 15-1.** Process for Sizing Graphics. Graphics should be sized to fit the space available while leaving white space.

For this reason most proposal shops ask the author to specify the figure's size when submitting a hand-drawn draft. The artist can then design the graphic to fit the designated space. The graphic form I've provided in Sample D requests this and other information that will allow graphics tracking.

**Example 6-6:** Sample Improperly Sized Figure

Sizing figures is one of the more challenging parts of creating them. In page-limited proposals, tables must also be tightly sized to prevent wasted space. The idea is to fill the space available while allowing some room—white space—to create a pleasing layout, as in Example 15-1. Too much white space, created by a figure that is poorly proportioned, makes for an awkward layout, as in Example 15-2.

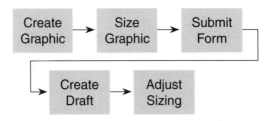

**Figure 15-2.** Process for Sizing Graphics. Graphics that are inappropriately sized look awkward on the page.

For this reason most proposal shops ask the author to specify the figure's size when submitting a hand-drawn draft. The artist can then design the graphic to fit the designated space. The graphic form I've provided in Sample D requests this and other information that will allow graphic tracking.

**Exploring Your Graphics Software**

In the "old days," both figures and tables were created in graphics programs. Today, tables are normally created in word-processing software; figures are created in graphics software, using anything from high-end products like Adobe® Illustrator® to Claris MacDraw®, Microsoft® PowerPoint®, or Corel DRAW®.

As I noted in the beginning of this section, I've never seen the advantage of the higher-end products and feel that they afford one major disadvantage: few people know how to use them, so you can be forced to hire a consultant if your sole graphics artist becomes ill or leaves for vacation in the middle of a proposal. However, most professional illustrators prefer high-end packages because they offer advanced features that can be used to develop other forms of corporate art, such as glossy marketing materials.

Whatever your preferred graphics program, I advise the proposal coordinator to become familiar with its features and capabilities. You want to be able to direct the proposal artist if necessary. You also don't want to be surprised to discover that you can't do what you thought you could do. Hands-on experience is best, but skimming through the manual will do nicely, too.

Creating tables in a graphics program has some advantages:

- You can better achieve a consistency of style among tables and graphics if they are all created in the same program.

- Tables are sometimes easier to shrink to a smaller size when created in a graphics program.

Weigh those advantages when deciding how your proposal will be produced.

**Developing a Graphics Style**

The reproduction process dictates some of the limitations of graphics styles. Very dark grayscale shadows and lots of black tend to smudge in the copier. Light grayscales tend to fade. Dark graphics also draw attention to themselves, throwing off the page balance. For this reason, graphics that might work fine in a slide presentation are inappropriate for proposals.

Many years ago, I worked with a truly outstanding artist who both spoiled me and defined my preferred graphics style forever. He used a medium grayscale to create drop shadows behind boxes, a sans serif font for figure text, stylized representations of computer and humans, and curved lines instead of straight wherever he could. The result was a work of art that also conveyed technical information.

Today's clip art is far superior to what was available at that time and can actually be used in proposals without embarrassment. But I still shy away from representations of humans that look like cartoons or computer representations that attempt too much detail. Stylized figures add a touch of class without loss of meaning, as Example 6-7 shows.

**Example 6-7:** Sample Stylized Figures

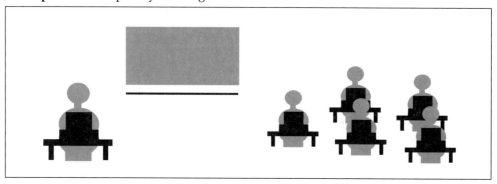

### Preparing for Oral Presentations

In Chapter 11, I discuss oral presentations, which are another kind of animal altogether. When you're preparing for a written proposal and a presentation at the same time, keep in mind that what will work on the printed page may not work on a slide. Review your graphics one by one to see if you need to change a graphic for the presentation.

### Tracking Proposal Graphics

I've been exposed to several methods of tracking graphics through the proposal process, and some are more complex than others. The simplest is illustrated in Example 6-8.

**Example 6-8:** Sample Graphics Tracking System

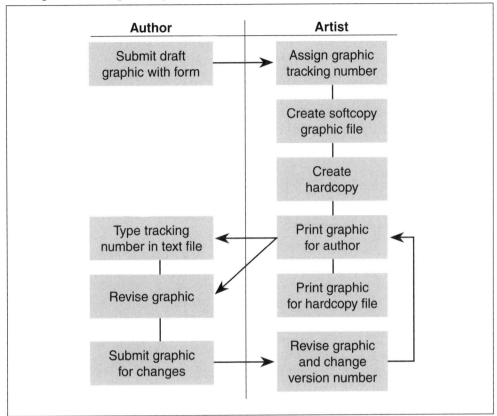

In this method, a writer submits a draft of a proposed graphic using a form such as the one provided in Sample D. The artist then follows these steps:

- *The artist assigns a tracking number to the graphic, for example, CAR0001v1, CAR0002v1, CAR0003v1, CAR0004v1.* In this example, the first three characters identify the proposal; the last four identify the graphic. These seven characters comprise the tracking number. The final two characters identify the *version number.* All graphics begin at v1. As authors and editors make changes, the version number ascends sequentially.

- *The artist creates a physical file folder and a soft-copy file, each named using the assigned tracking number (omitting the version number).* The soft-copy file holds the computer-generated graphic. The physical file stores the form on which the draft graphic was submitted and all subsequent versions of the graphic as they are made.

- *The artist types the tracking number in the soft-copy file.* In the soft-copy file, the artist types the tracking number and the version number in small type at the bottom of each graphic. Each printout of the graphic thus displays both tracking and version numbers.

- *The artist changes the version number.* As the artist makes changes to a graphic, she increases the version number typed in the soft-copy file by one number and places a copy of the computer printout into the physical file.

- *The author types the tracking number in the text file.* When the author receives the first computer-generated copy of the graphic, he types the tracking number into the appropriate location in his text file so that each figure cited in the proposal narrative is associated with a tracking number.

- *The proposal coordinator matches the tracking numbers.* The proposal coordinator matches the tracking numbers in the text files and with those on the graphics to assemble review copies of the proposal, as I describe further in Chapter 10.

- *If an author abandons use of a particular graphic, she removes the tracking number from the text file.* No action is necessarily required on the part of the artist unless many graphics are deleted. In this case, the artist may want to remove the physical file folder from the active filing system to an inactive system and place the soft-copy file in an inactive directory or folder.

By doing this, the artist saves himself the work of printing soft-copy graphics that are no longer in service. The proposal coordinator also has a second method of confirming—other than talking with the author—that graphics that can't be matched with tracking numbers in the text file are no longer active.

This system also works for tracking the occasional hand-drawn graphic, letter, spreadsheet printout, or similar oddball items that often make their way into proposals. Because they *are* oddball items, authors forget how to handle them. So it's the proposal coordinator's responsibility to follow up, ensuring that oddball items are assigned tracking numbers and are stored in a physical file folder, thus becoming part of the tracking system. Eventually, oddball graphics must be pasted in place for the final production, unless your artist scans them into the soft-copy system. I talk about this option below.

### Tracking Graphics for Large Proposals

If your proposal is very large and several artists are creating the graphics, you may need an additional person just to track the graphics. This person assigns tracking numbers for the artists, makes sure that the artist increases the version number with each change, and manages the physical filing system. He can also maintain a three-ring binder that holds the most recent version of each graphic. Under these conditions, the graphics coordinator makes a copy of each new version of a graphic for the writer, the physical file folder, and the three-ring binder.

### Scanning Oddball Graphics into the System

You can make production easier if you scan oddball graphics into the soft file system. I've seen artists scan in letters, signatures, and graphics from incompatible systems that for one reason or another cannot or should not be recreated on the in-house graphics software. The result is a final proposal printout that is paste-up free.

Amazingly, as software has evolved, very little about the production process has changed in any substantive way. In fact, as color printers become the standard and color graphics or digital pictures find their way into proposals, we are simply stepping up to the next level of complexity and creating more stylistic and software compatibility issues that must be addressed before the production process begins.

When you envision the final proposal document and plan in advance how you will arrive at that document without the frustration of needless rework, you will reduce stress for the technical team, the production staff, and yourself.

# CHAPTER 7

# *Gearing Up*

If your proposal process is working, you and the capture manager should be planning the proposal long before the RFP is released. This entails holding at least one planning meeting during which you'll want to exchange the following types of information. Make sure that you schedule the meeting or meetings to allow plenty of time to establish rapport and cover all necessary topics.

## GATHERING INFORMATION

The capture manager is often a visitor in the proposal shop in the same way that the rest of the proposal team is. Frequently, she is also the highest ranking technical manager working on a proposal effort and carries the authority of that position. It is therefore critical to engage the capture manager in the attitudes you want to project and the processes the team will use so that you and she will be acting in concert rather than in contention.

Don't assume that any capture manager—no matter how long he has been with the company—understands how the process works. Explain the following in detail:

- Your attitudes about proposals and your agenda to create this winning proposal in a stress-free environment.

- The proposal coordinator's roles in providing support and managing the process, using one of the models in Chapters 2 and 3 or another of your design.

- The capture manager's role in managing development and expressing the proposal solution, using the model cited in the bullet above.

- The process in its entirety, making certain that the capture manager understands how the responsibilities will be divided up and what you will do when. Use graphics and instructions developed in Chapter 4.

Use the following visual aids for your presentation:

- Examples of presentation slides for the kickoff meeting (Chapters 4 and 7)

- A sample schedule (see Example 7-18)

- Standardized forms (checklists and samples in appendices)

- A compliance/assignment matrix (Example 7-12) from a previous proposal.

Most capture managers will be relieved and grateful that you will be handling significant responsibility for the proposal so that they can focus on the technical solution. A few will want to do things the way they were done in another company at another time. Pick your fights carefully, while emphasizing that your proposal process is similar to methodologies for designing computer networks, software, health delivery systems, or educational programs. If you don't use the methodology, you won't achieve the results you want.

## ASKING THE RIGHT QUESTIONS

Ask every question that you can think of regarding the capture manager's plans for the proposal:

### Who will your technical resources be, where are they located now, and where will they be located for the proposal effort?

You want to know where your technical resources are located now so that you can distribute the RFP immediately when it arrives. From the answer to this question, you can also determine your requirements for the items listed below:

- Office space

- Computers

- Passwords

- E-mail

- Telephones.

The number of contributors is more important than who they are, but you'll want to know if any team employees will be working in your offices. Remember that teammates sometimes pose security risks, particularly when the team is working in tight quarters that are possibly stocked with old proposals and proprietary information. I've been in situations where a teammate on one proposal was a competitor on a concurrent effort. Provide a warm welcome, but make certain that server access is limited appropriately and proprietary information is out of reach.

### What is the predicted turnaround time?

Use the answer to this question to work backward from the due date to develop a preliminary schedule. More about this later.

### Is there a possibility of rewriting boilerplate, résumés, or past performance data before the RFP is released?

Particularly when you are competing again for a contract that you've already held or know a lot about, you have the possibility of updating résumés, rewriting old boilerplate, or touching up past performance data before the RFP is released.

This is a judgment call that depends on how much you know about the impending RPF and how much you're willing to risk. I've rewritten an entire management section before the RFP release, and much of it was worthless afterwards. On other efforts, we've gotten a substantial head start on résumés and past performance, all of which was useable.

### What support does the capture manager want in terms of writers, editors, word-processors, and technical illustrators?

An experienced capture manager will have assessed the writing skills of his primary technical participants. One of my favorite technical leaders was dyslexic and needed a translator to convert his material to standard English. Others are superb writers who provide near-perfect narrative, ready for production. If the capture manager hasn't done his homework, assume that substantive editors and copyediting are necessary. Push for more information on writing support.

Consult with the production manager about availability of staff and the need for temporary employees. If you are responsible for securing proposal consultants or assigning writers, inform them of the requirement and check their availability.

If you're using temporary employees at any level, remember to provide them with confidentiality agreements and make necessary arrangements with your corporate offices. Many companies require an employer identification number (EIN) of consultants on file. Experienced proposal coordinators collect the EINs and the hourly rates of a number of consulting companies so that they can call on those companies when a proposal begins.

***Who are your corporate teammates, and who are the individuals who will serve as their point persons?***

If you are teaming with other companies, call the point persons from those companies and ask for preliminary background materials. If you will need résumés and past performance information from other companies, start working to get them today.

## OUTLINING THE PROPOSAL AND CREATING A COMPLIANCE MATRIX

Sections C, L, and M of the RFP are most important to the technical and management volumes of the proposal.

When the RFP arrives, distribute it to your list of proposal contributors. If you receive a hard copy, scan Section C of the document and any other relevant specifications into a soft-copy format so that you can use it later. Then begin outlining the proposal.

### Examining Section C

Section C is normally a description of the job to be completed and typically includes an introduction explaining the mission and goals of the contracting organization, followed by a more detailed specification. Section C can be a set of technical specifications that might read something like Example 7-1.

**Example 7-1:** Sample Section C Specification (1)

> C.3.1.2. The offeror shall provide Macintosh- and Windows-compatible laptop computers, each with a minimum of the following features: 180 MHz processor, 16 MB ram, 1 GB of hard disk storage, 8X CD ROM, and internal 28.8 baud modem.
>
> C.3.1.3. The offeror shall provide a networking operating system compatible with Macintosh, UNIX, and Windows environments.

Or, it can be a description of services to be performed, such as in Example 7-2.

**Example 7-2:** Sample Section C Specification (2)

C.4.5.2. The offeror shall provide all the equipment and staffing necessary to respond to 1,000 medical hotline calls per week.

C.4.5.3. The offeror shall analyze requirements for microcomputer and communications hardware and software, develop specifications for any additional components required, establish and maintain files regarding requirements, and plan for and accomplish required network and workstation relocations.

Sometimes Section C also contains a set of management responsibilities, as Example 7-3 illustrates.

**Example 7-3:** Sample Section C Management Requirements

C.5.9.1. The offeror's program manager shall attend monthly oversight meetings with the government's contract representative.

C.5.9.2. The offeror shall provide monthly cost accounting following the format shown in Attachment 3.

## Examining Section L

Section L normally includes broad requirements for the contents and format of the proposal, as Example 7-4 illustrates.

**Example 7-4:** Section L Volume Requirements

L.2.1 The proposal shall contain three volumes under separate binders, as follows:

L.2.1.1 Volume I—Technical/Management. The technical proposal shall contain the offeror's technical and management approaches to the contract requirements.

L.2.1.2 Volume II—Past Performance. The Past Performance volume shall contain the past performance data.

L.2.1.3 Volume III—Cost. The Cost volume shall contain the offeror's proposed costs, along with a completed set of representations and certifications.

L.3 The offeror shall submit copies in the following numbers:

　Volume I—Technical/Management: 7 copies
　Volume II—Past Performance: 5 copies
　Volume III—Cost: 3 copies

Occasionally the government asks for "sanitized" copies of the cost volume. This means that all cost information must be "whited out" in some way, leaving all the other data in place. Even if you are not responsible for the cost volume, this is a production issue that you may need to plan for down the road.

The government also frequently limits the pages in each of the narrative volumes. For example, the technical/management volume might be limited to 150 pages and the past performance volume limited to 15 pages. On the other hand, some bids aren't limited at all. The largest bid I worked on included five 5-inch volumes of text with 17 volumes of documentation.

Section L also contains stipulations on the proposal's format, as shown in Example 7-5.

**Example 7-5:** Sample Section L Formatting Requirements

L.4.1.1. Proposals shall be submitted on 8.5 x 11 pages with single-spaced text in 12-point Times or Times New Roman font. Fold-out pages to a maximum of 11 x 17 inches may be used judiciously and shall be numbered as two pages, for example, II - 25/26. Pages shall be numbered sequentially within each volume, for example, I - 1, I - 2, I - 3 through I - 125.

L.4.1.2. One copy of each volume shall be submitted in Microsoft Word for Windows format on a single 3.5-inch disk. Illustrations may be omitted.

No matter how ugly the proposal will be, you must follow these instructions to the letter. As Example 7-6 illustrates, the government normally explains its expectations for each volume in greater detail later in Section L.

The examples I use here are simplistic. Often the volume instructions consume several detailed pages. Detail is good, because the more detail, the better guidance you have.

Other possible pieces of Section L include the address to which the proposal must be delivered; the location and hours of operation of a bidder's library; security or subcontracting requirements; and assumptions that the offeror must use in costing the proposal (such as how many trips should be used for estimating travel or how much should be added to the budget for required leases).

Another standard piece in Section L is a statement that the offeror should not be overly lavish in producing the proposal. Ignore this statement unless you were planning to inlay your graphics with gold. You want to present the best proposal that you can, including simple, direct narrative and complementary graphics. I have never known a company to be disqualified for going overboard.

**Example 7-6:** Sample Section L Requirements for Proposal Volumes

---

2.0 Volume 1—Technical/Management. In this volume the offeror shall describe the approach to and management of the contract, including methodologies and tools.

2.1 Technical Approach. Describe how you will complete the requirements of the contract, including methodologies for maintaining software, programming new software, and responding to user requests. Explain your approach to developing and maintaining networked systems, including monitoring performance, planning for increased or decreased capacity, administering passwords and permissions, and managing system failures.

2.2 Management Approach. Describe your corporation's chain of command and the methods and procedures you will use to staff the contract and resolve problems. Name the key personnel, their qualifications, and their roles, as you see them. Explain your corporation's cost accounting tools, methods, and procedures.

3.0 Volume II—Past Performance. Provide the following information for each of the contracts you have worked on for the past three years:

    Contract Name
    Contract Number
    Contracting Agency
    Government Contracting Officer/Phone
    Company Project Manager/Phone
    Contract Beginning and End Dates
    Contract Cost at Award
    Contract Cost at Completion
    Explanation of Difference
    Narrative Description of the Work Completed

4.0 Volume III—Cost. The Cost volume shall be divided into three sections: Representations and Certifications, Exceptions, and Proposed Cost.

---

## Examining Section M

Section M contains the evaluation factors that will be used to evaluate your proposal and weigh its value against other proposals. Normally Section M states the criteria that will be used and the weight of each of the volumes, as in Example 7-7.

**Example 7-7:** Sample Section M Evaluation Factors

M.2.1. The following weights will be applied to the proposal volumes:

- Technical Management: 50 percent
- Past Performance: 15 percent
- Cost: 35 percent

M.2.1.1. Technical/Management: The Technical/Management volume will be evaluated by answering the following questions: Did the offeror clearly, thoroughly, and specifically describe the approach that will be taken to complete work under this contract? Did the offeror adequately describe the methodologies and tools that will be used? Did the offeror explain the corporate hierarchy and the methods and procedures that will be used to staff the contract and to revolve problems? Did the offeror describe the methods, procedures, and tools used for cost accounting?

M.2.1.2 Past Performance: The Past Performance volume will be evaluated by answering the following questions: Did the offeror thoroughly and accurately describe the past performance for the last three years? Did the references contacted present a collaborating view with respect to the work performed and the quality of performance?

M.2.1.3. Cost: The Cost volume will be evaluated by answering the following questions: Does the proposed cost seem reasonable for the services or products to be provided, as stated in the Section C specification? As outlined in the Technical/Management proposal?

## Combining Sections C, L, and M

The trick in outlining the proposal is to capture all the information in sections C, L, and M into a single outline. In most instances, you start with the Section L outline and fit Sections C and M into it. However, sometimes Section L seems to zero in on an itsy-bitsy area of Section C, and it's best to cover Section C completely while working Section L into the outline.

To continue the example used above, assume that Section C is a detailed specification, and your instructions in Section L are those shown in Example 7-7. Your best bet would be to outline Section C, creating a major section for each of the major products or services that the contract covers. Then weave into that outline subsection titles that show an obvious relationship to Section L, as shown in Example 7-8.

Again, these examples are simplistic, although I must say that the evaluation factors are sometimes amazingly vague. Sometimes Section M tracks exactly with the Section L outline, while other times it introduces entirely new words and concepts, exasperating even the most experienced outliner.

**Example 7-8:** Sample Section Titles

Methodology and Tools for Maintaining Software

Methodology and Tools for Programming New Software

Methodology and Tools for Responding to User Requests

Approach to and Tools for Developing and Maintaining Networked Systems
—Monitoring Performance
—Planning for Increased or Decreased Capacity
—Administering Passwords and Permissions
—Managing System Failures

As with technical sections, name the management sections to reflect a direct relationship with Section L, as illustrated in Example 7-9. If Section C contains management requirements, weave them into the Section L requirements.

**Example 7-9:** Sample Section Headings

Corporate Chain of Command

Methods and Procedures for Contract Staffing

Methods and Procedures for Resolving Problems

Key Personnel, Qualifications, and Roles

Cost Accounting Tools, Methods, and Procedures

## Creating Headings

If sections or subsections of the RFP do not have headings, you must create them. I prefer using active verbs in the gerund form (that is, ending with "ing") followed by a noun, as in the headings for this manual. If the government has provided some headings and omitted others, it is best to maintain consistency with the government's format, as in Example 7-10.

**Example 7-10:** Sample Requirement and Section Heading

**Section C Requirement:** C.7.4.10 Develop and maintain, as a minimum, the following procedure manuals: System Recovery Plan, LAN Maintenance Guide, LAN Troubleshooting Guide, Workstation Installation/Relocation Guide, New User Information Package, Out-Processing Guidelines, Peripheral Equipment Instruction Sheets.

**Proposal Heading:** I.2.7.4.10 Developing and Maintaining Procedure Manuals

Use your judgment in choosing how you will address lower-level Section C requirements. For example, in Example 7-10 the government mentions seven types of manuals. These manuals could be addressed in unnumbered subsections, in bullet form, or in a table.

## Numbering the Outline

It is sometimes possible to number the proposal outline and then the proposal itself in a way that tracks directly with Section C or L. For example, if the Section C specifications begin at C.3, you may be able to set up your technical volume so that Section I.1 is, for example, an Executive Summary; Section I.2 is an Introduction; and Section I.3 begins your response to the individual pieces of the specification. In this way, your technical response could track exactly with Section C, as in Example 7-11.

**Example 7-11:** Sample Matching of Section C and Proposal Outline

---

**Section C Outline**

| | |
|---|---|
| C.1 | Scope of Work |
| C.2 | Background |
| C.3 | Statement of Work |
| C.3.1 | Furnishing Personnel, Materials, and Facilities |
| C.3.2 | Providing and Managing Resources |
| C.3.3 | Task 1: Application Software Support |
| C.3.3.1 | Assisting Staff in Maintaining and Using Databases |

**Example Proposal Outline**

| | |
|---|---|
| I.1 | Executive Summary |
| I.2 | Introduction |
| I.3 | Response to Statement of Work |
| I.3.1 | Furnishing Personnel, Materials, and Facilities |
| I.3.2 | Providing and Managing Resources |
| I.3.3 | Task 1: Application Software Support |
| I.3.3.1 | Assisting Staff in Maintaining and Using Databases |

---

One very large, well-known customer broke the numbering scheme in the middle of the proposal and picked up the Section C numbering. I don't subscribe to this method of tracking Section C, but people do it. The proposal wasn't rejected for non-compliance or silly numbering.

## Checking Other Sections

Always inspect the RFP from cover to cover to locate other sections and attachments that affect the proposal outline at the section or subsection level.

For example, Section H contains a description of special contract requirements, such as those related to travel, maintenance, and key personnel. (In Example 7-9, for example, you would fit the titles of key personnel under the heading "Key Personnel, Qualifications, and Roles.") Section J often contains attachments that define the contract deliverables, the customer's hardware and software, and pertinent system specifications.

If you spot something that looks important as you read, flag it. Technical staff are frequently inexperienced at proposal writing and may not read the RFP from cover to cover, even when the profess that they have. Bring questionable material to the capture manager's attention so that he can resolve the issue.

## Creating a Compliance Matrix

A *compliance matrix* is a table showing where in the proposal you have addressed the government's Section C, L, and M requirements. An *assignment matrix* identifies the individuals who hold primary responsibility for proposal sections and proposal milestones. Use your outline to develop a working compliance and assignment matrix that looks something like Example 7-12.

**Example 7-12:** Sample Compliance and Assignment Matrix

| Volume/ Section | Title | Section C Reference | Section L Reference | Pages | Section M Reference | Writer |
|---|---|---|---|---|---|---|
| Vol I | Technical/Management | n/a | L.2 | 150 | M.2 | n/a |
| I.1 | Executive Summary | n/a | n/a | 2 | n/a | Linda J. |
| I.2 | Introduction | | | 7 | | Joe M. |
| I.3 | Response to Statement of Work | C.3 | L.2 | .5 | M.2 | Maria O. |
| I.3.1 | Designing Computer Networks | C.3.1 | L.2 | 1 | M.2 | Maria O. |
| 1.3.1 | Maintaining Computer Systems | C.3.2 | L.2 | 1 | M.2 | Maria O. |

Note that in Example 7-12, the first column is the volume and section number; the second, the volume or section title; and the third, the Section C reference.

When the RFP expressly requests a compliance matrix and defines its format in Section L, the requirement sometimes specifies that the first column holds the Section C requirement. If you are bidding hardware and software systems, you may independently choose to follow the same strategy to emphasize your compliance with all the Section C requirements. In this case, you can place the Section C number and the full text of the requirement in the first two columns on the left. In other cases, the Section C reference appropriately follows the section title and a number, and an abbreviated form of the requirement is adequate.

If you have a soft copy of the RFP, use it to cut and paste section numbers and requirements into the matrix, where appropriate.

Eventually you can turn this matrix into a schedule by adding columns for various due dates or activities and filling them in as the proposal progresses. You can also use it as the final compliance matrix by deleting the columns related to section assignments and the proposal schedule. If you update it as changes are made—and they will be—you will have saved yourself lots of energy when production begins.

Speaking of changes, don't take changes to your outline or compliance matrix personally. One of the functions of the proposal coordinator is to put on paper her best guess of what the outline or matrix should be so that others can criticize it. People often need an example to jog their own thinking. Nevertheless, make certain that changes affecting compliance or interrupting common sense are thoroughly reviewed and justified. Proposal outlines are often a matter of interpretation, and some people's interpretative skills are decidedly better than others'.

## COLLECTING MORE INFORMATION

The government usually provides two standard opportunities to gather more information about a bid once the RFP is released. One is the pre-bid conference. The other is providing for a written response to questions submitted by bidders within a specified period of time. The government collects questions from bidders and responds in writing, distributing the responses to all bidders so all can see the questions asked and the government responses.

## Attending the Pre-bid Conference

Pre-bid conferences can vary greatly. Those I've attended have been unrevealing, with government employees simply repeating information from the RFP. Others I've heard about through the grapevine seemed to have provided greater technical detail or hints about what technical solution would be preferred—at least in the retelling. In most cases, substantive questions posed to the government at the pre-bid conference were answered after the conference with other questions that had been submitted directly to the government through the mail, e-mail, or fax.

If the pre-bid conference is within driving distance, it's a good idea for the proposal coordinator to attend. The conference is another opportunity to uncover hidden customer needs; the more ears listening, the better. Technical personnel tend to focus on technical information, overlooking aspects of the conference that might affect the outline, marketing strategy, win themes, discriminators, or production. If the proposal coordinator cannot attend the conference, he should ask an attendee to listen for information about any area of his concern.

## Submitting Written Questions

Work closely with technical contributors to elicit questions from them. Also, prepare all questions, particularly those affecting the proposal outline, format, or production. Example 7-13 provides a standard format.

**Example 7-13:** Sample Written Question

> Question 1: With reference to Section C.3.2.1.5, the government does not define the type of processor to be provided with microcomputer workstations. Is this an oversight, or are offerors free to propose as they wish?

Before submitting questions, edit them for clarity and check all citations. If you don't understand what is being asked or can't find a cited section of the RFP, the government won't be able to either.

Don't be afraid to submit a question on any aspect of the proposal that you or a colleague finds vague or incomprehensible. The worst that will happen is the government will write a condescending response, in which case you say a few choice words under your breath, make a best guess at what they want, and move on.

Also, consider the possibility that some questions are better left unasked. If you will have more flexibility in your response without shedding new light on an issue, you might refrain from submitting a question to the government. You might also omit questions that suggest—even in an oblique way—the direction you're taking in your proposal solutions. Confer with your capture manager about the ramifications of asking questions whose answers might have the potential to cause more harm than good, remembering that all bidders will be reading all questions and responses.

Some companies use questions as a method to extend the proposal deadline. The notion is to ask every question possible in the hopes that the government will need to extend the deadline to answer the questions. This strategy has been known to work, and it can be particularly advantageous for a challenger to an incumbent offeror. The incumbent offeror generally benefits from a fast turnaround time, in that it is normally most familiar with the customer and can offer up a ready solution, while a challenging offeror must create a solution from scratch.

Questions also apply to draft RFPs. I recently worked on a proposal from an agency that had issued a draft RFP before the final RFP was posted. Because I was busy completing another proposal, I glanced at the draft but didn't submit questions during the draft phase. I regretted my negligence later, when I had issues about the requirements for proposal submission and the evaluation factors.

Although I wasn't required in any way to review and question the draft, I think that the government would have been more receptive to my questions and more willing to clarify issues if the questions had been submitted during the draft phase. Once the real RFP is on the street, the government is aware of stalling tactics and can be stubborn in its refusal to clarify vague requirements.

## HOLDING THE KICKOFF MEETING

The kickoff meeting is the single most important event in the proposal process, but you wouldn't know this from the ones I've attended. At the kickoff meeting, the proposal coordinator sets a tone, provides authors with the big picture, explains the proposal process, and introduces people who will be communicating with each other at a later date. The goal of the meeting is to make sure that participants have a common understanding of where they are going and how they're going to get there.

If the proposal team doesn't emerge from the kickoff meeting with a common understanding, you will probably regret it later. On one job for a small company rebidding its keystone contract, the proposal team consisted of consulting writers and on-staff managers. Several weeks into the job and long after a pep-rally-like kickoff meeting, we realized that the writers and managers had differing views of what was being proposed. The consultants were writing to RFP requirements for the new contract; the managers were speaking to the way things worked on the current contract. We had to redo much material before the corporate officers honored our request to call a full team meeting. Some writers had to return nearly to the beginning in developing their sections.

**Preparing for the Evaporation Factor**

The kickoff meeting should be mandatory for the entire design team. If you want to warn tangential personnel, such as an entire staff of a small company, about what is coming down the pike and give them the basics of your strategy, it should be done in another meeting.

The kickoff meeting should be a serious matter reserved for the proposal team that is perfectly planned and meticulously executed because—and this is a big because—after the kickoff meeting, major participants have been known to vanish. They disappear to places that can be reached only by e-mail and are heard from only after 20 increasingly nasty dispatches.

The kickoff meeting should include, at a minimum, the following:

- Introduction of teammates and proposal team

- Preview of the agency and the procurement

- Highlights of the proposed solution

- Major discriminators

- Review of the proposal process

- Proposed writing assignments

- Proposed schedule.

You will need an overhead projector, prepared slides, and a room that's big enough to hold the entire team. Let your teammates know ahead of time that this is a mandatory meeting, and ask senior-level managers to convey this expectation firmly. Then begin work on the following items.

### Introducing the Proposal Team

With the capture manager, prepare a slide that lists all teammates by company, showing what each brings to the table, as illustrated in Example 7-14. List the names of participants from teammate companies, including their titles and primary skills.

**Example 7-14:** Sample Teammate Slide

| | |
|---|---|
| **Lisner Associates, Inc.**<br>**818 Springhill Road**<br>**McLean, Virginia 22102**<br>**(703) 993-2456** | Woman-owned 8(a) with network support experience at the FAA. |
| Doris Lisner | President and Point Person |
| John Wilson | Network Design, Development, Administration |
| **Kashanian & Company, Inc.**<br>**1037 16th Street, N.W.**<br>**Washington, D.C. 20009**<br>**(202) 673-2437** | Medium-sized company with strong wireless communications credentials |
| Tom Rounder | Manager, Government Services, Point Person |
| Leslie Davenport | Wireless communications and beeper services |
| **Shore Wireless**<br>**1847 Easton Parkway**<br>**Cambridge, Maryland**<br>**(410) 786-7836** | Manufacturer of cellular phones and beepers |
| Dan Howard | Account Executive, Federal Government Division, and Point Person; cellular phone and beeper specifications |

Prepare a slide similar to Example 7-15 to present your in-house team along with their positions and capabilities. Also, prepare a handout with contact numbers for each team member.

**Example 7-15:** Sample Proposal Team Slide

| Name | Position | Expertise | Location | Contact Numbers |
|---|---|---|---|---|
| Joe Smith | Capture Manager | Hardware & software systems development/ maintenance | 3300 Greenbelt Road | (301) 994-3400 Jsmith@gorg.com fax: (301) 994-3422 |
| Anne Gordon | Proposal Coordinator | Proposal development/ production | 3300 Greenbelt Road | (301) 994-3402 agordon@gorg.com fax: (301) 994-3422 |

### Previewing the Agency and Procurement

Again with your capture manager, prepare a set of slides that provides background information on the agency and the procurement. For example, you might provide the following two slides of background information:

- *The Agency.* Background information on the agency, such as the size, location of offices, important managers, mission, and long-term goals, particularly those related to this procurement.

- *The Procurement.* Major procurement requirements, with emphasis on *driving requirements* and *hot buttons* that are not available in the RFP.

Driving requirements acquire their name because they drive major choices pertinent to your proposed solution. For example, if the government is asking for a minicomputer-based system that includes a transaction processor, and the only transaction processor that meets the government requirements for number of transactions per minute runs only on minicomputer XYZ, then the requirement associated with the number of transactions in effect drives the overall system design.

To use a management example, assume you are rebidding on a job for which your current complement of management staff includes a project manager and four division managers for software, networked systems, help desk response, and operations. In the new RFP, the government breaks the support requirements into three areas: software, operations (under which it includes the help desk response), and networking. Thus, the requirement for three support areas drives the management structure. Driving requirements are particularly important to the entire team because they often have broad implications for other areas of the proposal.

*Hot buttons* are customer biases for or against certain products, methods, or procedures. For example, some agencies are well known for preferring non-verbal communications media, such as e-mail and memos. Others couldn't care less. Such biases are often not evident or are very subtle in the RFP; they nevertheless have important implications regarding features and benefits, discussed later. Share this information with your team.

### Highlighting the Proposed Solution

Provide an overview of your proposed system or service, highlighting major features and benefits. Even if your solution to the government's requirements is not fully fleshed out, provide what you can about the system or services to be offered, the management structure, and perhaps even the primary contracts that will be used to demonstrate relevant experience, even if past performance is not a part of the proposal outline.

A graphic is fine for presenting an overview of a large system or a management structure, but also provide a table of features and benefits, as in Example 7-16, so that other team members will start thinking features-benefits, features-benefits, features-benefits, ad nauseam. (Feature of husband: Great cook. Benefit to me: Delicious meals prepared while I work. Yum, yum, yum.) Features and benefits are described in detail in Chapter 8.

**Example 7-16:** Sample Features and Benefits Slide

| Feature | Benefit to Customer |
|---|---|
| Three linked XYZ minicomputers running DIPSY operating system, DOPSY transaction processor | Provides the capability to process 5,000 more requests per month than are currently processed |
| MOPSY network operating system, LOPSY routers and hubs, NOPSY servers | Offers the ability to communicate among all agency platforms transparently |
| 50 network, operations, and software staff with a combined 300 years of agency experience | Provides for smooth rollover from one contract to the next and continued participation of individuals who know the agency personnel, mission, and systems. |

## Dissecting the Competition

Prepare a slide listing the names of your primary competitors, their strengths and weaknesses, and major points that can be used to *ghost* their bids. *Ghosting* is a term for undermining a competitor's product or service without mentioning the competitor by name. If your competitor's product is faster than yours, while yours is more reliable, you can employ the meek approach of hammering home your reliability. Or, if you're bolder and have statistics to back up your assertion, you might include a table demonstrating that faster machines tend to have lower reliability.

If you know your competitor tends to hire engineers straight from school, while you employ highly experienced personnel, you might plan for strategic name-dropping in appropriate places about the important customer contracts that your employees have worked. ("Our engineers, who were essential to the design of mission control software for NASA's space station and the XYZ rocket, developed the company's proprietary software development and test methodology expressly for space-related software systems.") Your slide might look like Example 7-17.

**Example 7-17:** Sample Discriminators Slide

| Competitor | Bid/Company | Pros | Cons | Strategy |
|---|---|---|---|---|
| ABC Company | ABC mini-computers are the heart of the proposed system | Priced right system | Unreliable system | Our Mean Time Between Failure (MTBF) is 36 months; superior speed/reliability |
| | Huge corporation | Unending resources | Lack of account-ability at upper levels | Direct involvement of company executives |
| EFG Wireless | Upgrade of the system currently in use | The agency knows the system | Outdated interface | Introduction of an entirely new system presents an opportunity to update business processes along with the interface |

| Strong team with unusually tough-to-beat wireless capability | Incumbent | Poor service reputation | Demonstration of service record with previous clients, including commendations from X and T for repeatedly meeting one-hour response requirements |

Much of this type of material may have been prepared for presentation at a meeting in which the company's bid/no bid decision was made. If so, your job will be much easier.

## Explaining the Proposal Process

Explain your proposal process from start to finish using the examples in Chapter 4, which describe the proposal process, the anti-chaos theory, and your strategy for working on the network. Let writers know what is available to them online and how files are borrowed and returned.

Provide a gross schedule showing the primary milestones, such as the storyboard review, Pink Team, Red Team, production, and delivery, as shown in Example 7-18.

**Example 7-18:** Sample Proposal Schedule Slide

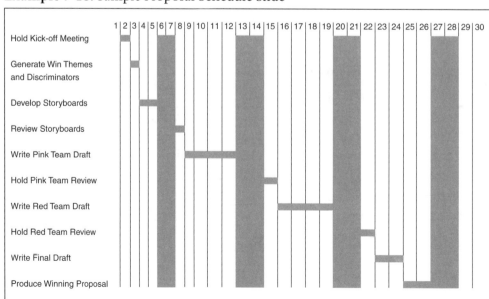

## Developing the Agenda

Given the prepared slides, your agenda for the kickoff meeting should look something like the list in Example 7-19. On the right, I have arbitrarily suggested times and proposed an individual who might present the associated material.

**Example 7-19:** Sample Kickoff Agenda

| Activity/Slides | Time | Proposed Presenter |
|---|---|---|
| Greeting | 1 minute | A Big Wig, such as the president of the company, if your company is a small organization; a vice president or division manager if your company is a large organization |
| The Proposal Team | 5 minutes | Big Wig |
| The Agency and Procurement | 10 minutes | Capture manager |
| The Proposed Solution | 20 minutes | Capture manager or technical lead |
| The Competition | 10 minutes | Capture manager |
| The Proposal Process and Philosophy | 10 minutes | Proposal coordinator |
| The Proposal Schedule | 5 minutes | Capture manager or proposal coordinator |

Big Wigs lend your proposal credibility, letting teammates know that this procurement is a company priority. The capture manager and technical lead have inside information on the bid that most participants don't yet and may never have, so they are essential. The proposal coordinator should present the proposal process as a subtle but important signal of authority (even if he has little).

## Designing the Handout

Your handout for the kickoff meeting should include copies of the slides the team has prepared, along with everything that will help a writer carry out his assignment. For example:

- *Past performance data.* Copy past performance data from earlier proposals, particularly summaries of earlier contracts having direct relevance. Don't overdo it, but give writers plenty of fodder for building your credentials.

- *Corporate data on teammates*. This can be copies of glossy brochures or past performance data that give a sense of the work your teammates have performed and their current clients.

- *Boilerplate*. Copy boilerplate on your company and its methodologies, with cover pages suggesting who might use it.

- *Sample graphics*. Some folks aren't used to developing graphics and need samples that show them the final look of your proposals, as discussed in Chapter 6.

- *Graphic submittal form*. See Sample D.

- *Style guide*. Style guides provide a format to follow and remind writers of common grammatical and stylistic mistakes. Sample B is an example.

Ponder, ponder, ponder what might be helpful down the line. I can't tell you the number of times that I've had to request information that should have been provided by those who know the company better than I. I'll be typing along and suddenly realize that the information I'm lacking *must have been* included in an earlier proposal. One time I specifically asked a manager of human resources for a review of the company's compensation plan, and she neglected to direct me to a full write-up, prepared within the last six months, which covered the entire plan. Duh?

It is part of the proposal coordinator's job to know what has been done before that needn't be done again. Rather than leaving this chore for some later date, do your homework now. It will save time later. Many of the items that you distribute at the kickoff meeting can become standard materials that you cull from and add to as needed (see Chapter 4).

## Presenting Your Slides

Supplement your slides with a practiced, polished delivery, because you can't enroll others in a process if you don't clearly stand for it yourself. Your knowledge of the details and expression of attitudes are your strongest tools for convincing others of the efficacy of your plan.

With your review of the process, emphasize the (new) proposal philosophy—that proposals can be orderly and enjoyable, rather than chaotic. Stress that team members will be held to their commitments not as a matter of principle but because holding individuals to their word will help to achieve the results you want—a winning proposal *and* a stress-free process.

# CHAPTER 8

# Building the Proposal Text

As is true with many of the topics covered in this book, proposal content could be addressed in a volume of its own. The components of a proposal and how they are constructed—along with the good, the bad, and the ugly of expository writing—have been addressed repeatedly in any number of books specific to the proposal process or general in approach. No author of a survey book such as this could presume to do more than to let the reader know that there is always more to learn on the topic of writing and persuasion.

Nearly every book about marketing—such as the results of research into why people buy—has some relevance to proposal writing. Nearly every book on writing provides some tidbit of technique that has some relevance to proposal writing. And even some books on basic business principles, addressing topics such as customer selection and focus, offer advice that can find its way into proposals.

Here I look at pieces of some proposals and offer only the most general of suggestions on how to assess their quality and improve on them.

## DEVELOPING WIN THEMES AND DISCRIMINATORS, THEME STATEMENTS, AND ACTION CAPTIONS

*Win themes* state the overarching features and benefits of your solution to the government's requirements. *Discriminators* state in a general way the advantages that your solution offers over that of your competitors. *Theme statements* summarize the most important features and benefits of your solution as they relate to a specific section or subsection of the proposal. *Action captions* summarize the most important features and benefits relative to a specific illustration.

If they remain valid as the proposed solution takes shape, win themes and discriminators often end up as elements of theme statements and action captions. They're also sprinkled throughout the proposal like fairy dust.

Win themes answer the question, "Why would *this* customer want to buy *this* product or service?" Discriminators answer the question, "Why would this customer want to buy this product or service *rather than* a competitor's product or service?" Win themes and discriminators set the stage for proposal contributors, giving them an overall context for the proposal narrative and for the theme statements and action captions that will be used throughout the proposal.

To answer the first question—"Why would *this* customer want to buy *this* product or service?"—you need to know your customer and your product. To answer the second question—"Why would this customer want to buy this product or service *rather than* a competitor's product or service?"—you need to know your customer, your product, your competitors, and their products. To answer both questions, you need to think in terms of features and benefits.

### Understanding Features and Benefits

Age-old sales wisdom says that people don't buy features, they buy benefits. *Features* are the physical attributes of your product or services; *benefits* explain their importance to the customers. People don't buy cars, they buy transportation; they don't buy refrigerators, they buy the ability to store perishable food. While the features-benefits rule is generally true, it may not always be applicable to government contracting.

In retail sales, the salesperson is presented with a customer who may or may not want to buy a product at all. In government contracting, the government obviously wants to buy a product or service, because the RFP says so. The job of the proposal team, guided by the capture manager and proposal coordinator, is to understand how the government wants to use this product or service and what it *values* in the contractor's delivery of the product or service. In other words, to prepare good government proposals, you need to understand what the customer wants *besides* the primary benefit offered by your product or service, because all your major competitors are selling the same primary item with the same primary benefit.

To work with the old example of refrigerators, assume that you are responding to an RFP for refrigerators. All competitors will be proposing to sell a brand of refrigerators to the government. Since all refrigerators preserve food, touting the ability to store food is a worthless sales strategy. To sell *this* customer your refrigerator you need to know what the customer is interested in besides storing food—space? status? energy savings? interior design? ease of use? price? a water dispenser? To sell *this* product, you need to know the physical characteristics of the product, all potential benefits of those characteristics, and the relative advantages of your product over those of competitors.

For example, I recently wrote a proposal to an agency within the Department of Defense. The proposal included a section on software coding, which would normally include a paragraph or so about adherence to software programming standards, such as those developed by Carnegie-Mellon's Software Engineering Institute. The proposing company was aware, however, that this particular agency tends to view standards as costly and even counterproductive. Consequently, we omitted mention of standards altogether. We could have mentioned them, but if we had done so, we would have had to overcome the government's known objections by proving that standards boost productivity and thus save money in the long run.

Answer the question, "Why would *this* customer buy *our* product or service?" with a statement such as, "Because we are the largest provider of wireless systems in the United States." Then define what "the largest provider" means in terms of the customer's work. If your customer is concerned about management accountability, your stature as the largest provider may translate into mature financial and management procedures and systems for exacting accountability.

Create a table like the one in Example 8-1, with features on the left and benefits on the right. Then drop the word "because" and combine the features and benefits to create a set of win themes. Now answer the question, "Why would this customer buy this product or service rather than our competitor's product or service?"

**Example 8-1:** Sample Features and Benefits

| Feature | Benefit |
|---|---|
| Because we are the largest provider of wireless communications services to U.S. and international companies | Mature financial and management procedures for government accountability |
| Because we employ a knowledgeable sales team with a combined 450 years of telecommunications experience | Ability to advise the customer on the right product for specific requirements—even those outside wireless communications |
| Because we have 20 major manufacturing subcontractors | Uninterrupted flow of stock to customer with no back orders |
| Because we have 14 local service personnel | 1-hour response to service requests |
| Because we have hand-over arrangements with major international carriers | Reliable wireless communication in major foreign countries |
| Because we offer 7 products with various advanced features | Ability to provide the right product for the right requirement rather than meeting all requirements with one product |

Again, use a "because" statement and translate that statement into benefits to the customer, as illustrated in Example 8-2.

**Example 8-2:** Sample Discriminators as Features and Benefits

| Feature | Benefit |
|---|---|
| Because we've been in business longer than all of our competitors | Reliability of products, services, and financial backing |
| Because our products have an average Mean Time Between Failure of 2 years, versus 1.5 years for XYZ company | Proven greater availability of wireless communication when needed |
| Because we have established relationships with wireless communication firms in most major urban settings | Availability of service in major U.S. cities |
| Because our staff includes telecommunication and networking specialists | We offer experience in every major wire and wireless medium to develop or execute an overall communication strategy suited to the customer's mission |
| Because we offer mature, written methods and procedures for all order and delivery processes | Customized written procedures will be available immediately at contract award so that you can begin ordering the next day |
| Because we offer an 800-number help desk staffed 24 hours a day | Free, immediate advice for ordering, using, and maintaining our systems |

You will note that win themes can be discriminators, and discriminators can be win themes. It is important to distinguish between the two—where there is a distinction—only because you can also use discriminators to ghost your competitors (see Chapter 7).

I tend to shy away from ghosting because it tends to involve negative statements, and I prefer to sell the government on positives rather than negatives. Some people, however, don't hesitate to take potshots at their competitors through statements such as, "Large companies cannot provide the kind of personalized service that our organization offers," or "Mainframe-based solutions offer little flexibility for future growth."

### Presenting Themes and Discriminators

Normally, you will present your first cut of the win themes and discriminators in features/benefits format at the kick-off meeting. If you have not had an opportunity to discuss them with the entire team or a significant subset thereof before the kick-off, you should do so shortly thereafter. Technical members of the proposal team often understand details of the solution that add up to big benefits for the customer, so their input should be solicited. Keep a file of the original themes and discriminators and update them as they evolve, distributing each iteration to the proposal team.

## Creating Theme Statements

Theme statements tie each section of the proposal to the overall win strategy. In many standard proposal formats, each section to a designated digit (for example, to the three-digit level, such as I.2.3 or I.3.2) begins with a theme statement. In the best proposals, the theme statements, when combined, cover all major points of a proposed solution. Theoretically, they can be plucked from the proposal narrative to form the executive summary. (I've never tried to do this, but you could probably identify the theme statements using an indexing capability and copy them from the proposal into a separate executive summary file.) Sometimes theme statements are separated from the rest of the text by special formatting or lines.

Theme statements should be tied to the win strategy while also reflecting the hierarchical structure of the proposal. That is, a theme statement for a section on servicing of wireless phones should be specific to servicing and should not mention topics covered in other sections, unless a tie-in to a related capability is part of the theme.

Some theme statements mimic win themes. As shown in Example 8-3, the theme statement for a section on servicing of wireless phones could directly repeat one or more of the win statements shown in Example 8-1.

**Example 8-3:** Sample Theme Statement

Our 14 local service specialists and national servicing subcontractors provide one-hour response to local service calls and prompt response in all major U.S. travel destinations.

## Creating Action Captions

An *action caption* is a sentence following a table or figure title that links some aspect of the table or figure to a direct benefit for the customer. Action captions are another opportunity to tie features with benefits and to hammer home your win themes. Consequently, they are a standard part of most proposals. An action caption for a methodology graphic, for example, links the best features of the methodology to specific benefits for the customer, as shown in Example 8-4.

**Example 8-4:** Sample Figure Title and Action Caption

> **Figure 22-4.** Shannon Associates' System Design Methodology. We interview managers, staff, and customers to capture requirements that are responsive to all users.

The point is to pull from the figure its most important meaning to the customer, thus guiding the customer in his interpretation of the figure.

## DEVELOPING STORYBOARDS AND DRAFTS

During the proposal process, the design team creates four versions of the proposal:

- The storyboard review version

- The Pink Team review version

- The Red Team review version

- The final production version.

The periods on each end of the proposal schedule, from the kick-off meeting to the storyboard review and from the Red Team review to final production, are relatively structured. The periods after the storyboard review until the Red Team review are less structured. The reasoning is that team members need a push to get off the ground, and the storyboarding process provides such a push. On the other end, the period between the Red Team review and final production is structured to ensure that all review comments find their way into the final document for on-time delivery.

In this chapter, I address the steps the proposal coordinator takes to facilitate the storyboarding process and to critique the proposal as it moves from review to review. I address the process for incorporating Red Team comments in Chapter 9 because that process is a logical outcome of the final review.

## Using the Modified Storyboarding Approach

Storyboarding was stolen from the movie industry many years ago, or so the story goes. It is a graphic-centered method for developing proposals by which the design team brainstorms to arrive at major points for each section of the proposal, develops central graphics, and writes theme statements with the goal of laying out all the proposal pages before the proposal is written. The storyboard layout is updated as the graphics and text evolve.

A classic storyboarding technique is posting the storyboards on a wall so that all members of the team can watch the proposal's progress. Contributors mark their comments and suggestions on the wall-based storyboards. This is a major advantage of storyboarding because it saves the team the hassle of compiling comments from various copies of the proposal.

Using storyboards in the way that they were originally intended—as a method for laying out and updating the entire proposal—is a great idea for small, page-limited proposals if two conditions can be met: (1) all members of the proposal team are working at one location, and (2) all the proposal contributors are sophisticated users of word processing or page layout software *or* the proposal team is supported by a dedicated word-processing staff.

Because these two conditions are rarely met in today's proposal environments, most companies use a modified storyboarding approach that is somewhat shy of the classic approach in both format and technique. The format, illustrated in Sample A, is akin to an illustrated outline, which is annotated with major themes and other characteristics, such as features and benefits. Many companies develop section storyboards in teams that are subsets of the entire design team and post the storyboards on the wall for review. Most companies don't lay out the entire proposal before writing.

The modified approach is content- rather than layout-based. That is, contributors attend to the content rather than to the actual layout of the proposal. This makes good sense, particularly if the proposal will be prepared in word-processing software and moved into desktop publishing software later in the process. It makes sense even if you will be producing the final proposal in word-processing software because high-cost design team members are less likely to spend too much time with the layout and too little time with the content.

The modified storyboard approach can be used in distributed or on-site team environments. If you have the opportunity, the space, and the time, however, I suggest that you use brainstorming sessions involving the entire design team to create the storyboards and later post them on a wall for review, as discussed in Chapter 9. In this way, all contributors start the proposal process with an overview of the entire proposal, preventing duplication of topics and promoting consistency of voice and theme.

If the proposal team can't be brought together, small teams or individuals can develop the storyboards, and they can be reviewed in the same manner as the Pink or Red Team review.

### Facilitating Storyboarding Sessions

If you choose a team approach to storyboarding, schedule daily brainstorming sessions during the first week of the proposal process, allowing time to work through all sections. Hold these sessions in a large room with an overhead projector, screen, and transparency markers. Then follow these steps:

- *Print each of the pre-formatted files created in Chapter 6.* Sample A is an example of a printed storyboard file.

- *Copy each of these files onto one or more overhead transparencies and reproduce all in hard-copy format as well, creating a set for each design team member.*

At the storyboarding meetings, follow these procedures:

- *Provide each design team member with a set of storyboard formats for all sections.*

- *Instruct the team members by relating to them the steps you will go through, as outlined below.*

- *Review the standard parts of the proposal: theme statements, figures, tables, action captions, and major points.* Remind the team to link features with benefits.

- *Ask each team member to serve as the leader for his assigned section.* Provide the leader with the transparencies for that section.

- *Ask design team members to review the section requirements and subheadings within the file, arriving at possible themes, major points, and figures.*

- *Following the rules of brainstorming, ask participants to withhold judgment of suggestions at brainstorming meetings.*

- *As you work through each section, the assigned leader writes suggestions on the transparency so all team members can see them.*

- *Serve as a facilitator for the storyboarding process.* Coach contributors on developing theme sentences, action captions, etc.

After the sessions, team members develop storyboards independently using the suggestions provided by their teammates, omitting ideas that seem inappropriate on second thought, and adding others. When the storyboards are completed, schedule uninterrupted wall reviews, as described in Chapter 9.

### Writing Drafts

After the storyboard review is completed, and between Pink and Red Team reviews, contributors write independently, expanding and refining the topics proposed in their storyboards. During this time, the proposal coordinator keeps abreast of progress through status meetings, described in Chapter 12, and informal proposal critiques, addressed below. Remind the proposal team to use the support materials created in Chapters 4 and 6, including the Style Guide (Sample B) and the Graphic Submittal Form (Sample D).

## CRITIQUING THE PROPOSAL

One of the proposal coordinator's roles in supporting the proposal process is critiquing the proposal for compliance and for writing that is at least passable. I rely on editors to fine-tune the writing because most of us have forgotten the vocabulary associated with talking about writing, if we ever learned it. Remember independent and dependent clauses, gerunds and participles, predicate adjectives and adverbs? It is extremely difficult to speak with someone about writing if both forget what those terms mean and lack the necessary vocabulary for conversation. Providing instructions about writing beyond examples of active and passive voice is out of the question for the same reason.

Fortunately, the subject of good writing has been covered by numerous authors, and plenty of good references are available. The following books are on my shelf:

- Jacques Barzun, *Simple and Direct: A Rhetoric for Writers*

- Claire Kehrwald Cook, *Line by Line: How to Edit Your Own Writing*

- William Zinsser, *On Writing Well*

- William Strunk, Jr. and E.B. White, *The Elements of Style*

- *The Chicago Manual of Style.*

I rely on basic writing texts because basic writing is what proposals should contain. I make few distinctions between good writing of any non-fiction variety and proposal writing, except that proposals contain fewer metaphors and similes.

Aside from writing, I see several major problems with proposals that are related to compliance:

- The writer is answering the wrong question.

- The writer is mentioning features without benefits.

- The writer is making assumptions about what the reader knows or doesn't know.

- The writer is missing or mixing big chunks of the story.

- The writer is burying major points.

The proposal coordinator should recognize these problems and point them out to writers as the proposal develops. Writers have long periods between reviews in which they can produce and refine narrative that doesn't answer the questions that the government is asking. You want to make sure that they remain on track between reviews by checking status, as addressed in Chapter 12, and by skimming the proposal on a regular basis.

You can do this if you keep an updated copy of each of the proposal volumes. Ask contributors to print their sections, collect them at stand-up meetings (see Chapter 12), and insert them into a binder.

## The Writer Is Answering the Wrong Question

Proposals answer two primary questions: "What?" as in, "What are you going to provide?", and "How?" as in, "How are you going to provide it? ("it" being a product, service, or both). "When" and "where" are most often prescribed by the government and are thus beside the point.

A common mistake of new proposal writers is to answer the question "How?" as though they were answering the question "What?" Rather than describing an approach and all the methods, procedures, and tools used to support that approach, the writer describes what is going to be provided.

Technical personnel often tend to forget the tools and techniques they use in their approach and focus instead on the outcome. To refocus the writer, ask questions that get specific responses:

- How do you model the system?

- Do you use modeling software?

- What software?

- How are the modeling results presented?

- What do you do with the results?

- How do the results feed into your design process?

## The Writer Is Mentioning Features without Benefits

Another common mistake, particularly among new writers in start-up companies, is offering generic approaches and procedures that are not customized for *this* customer—or for any other particular customer, for that matter. It is important to illustrate the benefits of the proposed features and to provide examples demonstrating how those features might work in the customer's environment. If this is impossible to do based on the available information and research, use examples from your other customers, as Example 8-5 illustrates.

**Example 8-5:** Using an Example from Another Customer

> In association with procedural changes, our image processor doubles production. After making small changes in pre-processing and post-processing procedures, for example, the XYZ corporation increased its output by 100 percent, from 500 to 1000 orders per week.

## The Writer Is Making Assumptions about the Reader's Knowledge

In the same way that writers tend to emphasize features and neglect benefits, they often fail to explain the meaning of features in a way that the customer can understand. As a result, technology-intensive proposals can end up reading like mail-order computer catalogues.

For example, many people know the name "Pentium," and they know that Pentium processors are fast. Assume that your competitors are offering a Pentium-based computer; you are bidding a no-name 180 MHz processor. You need to tell the customer how fast the 180 MHz processor is in relationship to what the customer knows—the Pentium. Is it as fast as the Pentium? Faster? In this example you are actually *ghosting* the competition at the same time that you're explaining your product. Once you have explained what you are bidding, you can then offer real-life benefits. Example 8-6 offers another illustration.

**Example 8-6:** Explaining the Features and Benefits

> Our 1.2 GB hard disk drive easily stores a set of standard office software in addition to the high-end, space-intensive graphics programs employed at the Agency. Used with the backup storage media that we propose, this drive represents a long-term investment that the Agency will not outgrow in the next several years.

A related problem is dropping the names of processes, forms, tools, and methods into the text without explaining what those methods are. Too much of this name-dropping leads me to believe that the writer is making up processes that don't exist. Any name of a process, form, document, or procedure deserves at least a one-phrase explanation. If you provide a full explanation for a name in one section and go on to cite the same name in other locations, its mention should be accompanied by a reminder of what it is. Example 8-7 provides illustrations.

**Example 8-7:** Explaining Processes, Forms, Documents, and Procedures

> Visiting nurses use the Healthmate program to track their cases. Healthmate, described fully in Section 3, is a database of online forms and standardized procedures that automates the case-tracking process.
>
> The Help Desk staff refer to our on-line Standard Operating Procedures when upgrading software. The Standard Operating Procedures are a set of step-by-step instructions for upgrading the agency's 35 standard programs on Windows and Macintosh computers. The staff locate the appropriate procedure using a keyword search, print the procedure, and carry it with them to the user's site for reference.

The writer doesn't have to explain every minute detail of the system or service design, just technical details and unusual aspects that will distinguish your bid from others.

### The Writer Is Missing or Mixing Big Chunks of the Story

You developed a proposal outline so that the final proposal will track closely with the RFP. Don't allow writers to drop or rearrange sections arbitrarily. Also make sure that even small elements of Sections C and L are addressed in some way, even if it's through a table or graphic. If the RFP mentions seven types of system documentation, from user manuals to system specifications, and each is not worthy of a separate paragraph, suggest a table that dissects their contents and check off the company's experience with each element of content.

### The Writer Is Burying Major Points

I pointed out elsewhere in this guide that I am a linear thinker whose mind naturally thinks in terms of first, second, and third points. The problem with this type of thinking and associated writing is that it can lead the writer to mention the most important points last: first we do this, then we do this, and the result is this. The result—often the most important point—ends up buried in the last sentence.

In good proposals, the writer grabs that information and positions it at the top of the paragraph or section in the theme statement or introductory material, so that the most important points are highlighted. Sometimes this is merely a matter of moving a sentence or paragraph as a block. On other occasions, the material must be rewritten to accommodate the reorganization. In a third scenario, the information must be provided at the beginning and end of a section.

## Writing Performance Metrics

Performance-based contracts are those for which the government or the contractor develops performance goals that must be met during the contract. These goals can range wildly depending on your industry, and no general discussion of them has much meaning without an industry context.

Generally, however, performance metrics are measurable performance goals that must be carefully crafted to make sure that you can meet them— while stretching. The performance metric must say what the goal is and how your company is going to track its performance against the goal. For example, a performance goal for a computer help desk may be to resolve 95 percent of all calls within one hour and to resolve the remaining five percent within four hours. A performance goal for a software development company may be to write 10,000 lines of code per month. A goal for a staffing company could be to fill each management opening within four weeks. For each of these metrics, you need to devise a process for tracking progress. For the help desk, you would probably use trouble ticket software that generates a time and date stamp when a ticket is opened and closed. Then it generates a summary report each month showing the percentages closed by the hour. The software development or staffing company would need similar processes. The emphasis, again, is not just on what you're going to do, but also on how you're going to do it.

## Matching the Solution to the Cost

In most organizations where I've worked as a consultant, the pricing specialist has been physically located in another section of the building, away from the proposal team. The analyst begins at some point to build the cost models according to the proposed solution, relying almost exclusively on counsel with the capture manager, who is then wholly responsible for ensuring that the text that supports this solution jibes with the cost model and the final total.

In the company where I'm currently working, two of the operations managers price the proposals. They work in the same location as the proposal team, and they are far more closely involved in the development of a technical solution than the pricing specialists described above. Nevertheless, we have had problems ensuring that the technical solution completely jibes with the price proposal.

It is incumbent on the proposal coordinator to remind the capture manager of her role in ensuring the consistency of the proposal across the technical and cost volumes. The proposal coordinator should pay particular attention to any portions of the technical proposal that address the issues of staffing, hardware, software, or other costly materials or services that the offeror is promising to provide to the government. Each should be costed in the price proposal.

If the capture manager changes the staffing in the technical proposal at the last minute, the proposal coordinator should be aware of the ramifications throughout the technical proposal and the general impact on the price proposal. You may not know exactly how and where the price proposal will change, but you should remind the capture manager that it will change.

If your workload is such that you and your capture manager cannot regularly review the proposal for writing quality, you will probably find yourself suffering during reviews.

To avoid that outcome, find someone on your team or hire a consultant to review the proposal as a whole for you.

# CHAPTER 9

# *Holding Proposal Reviews*

I can count on one hand the proposal reviews that I've attended that have been truly helpful to the proposal process and the proposal itself. At their worst, proposal reviews are so emotionally devastating that contributors can barely pull themselves together to complete their respective sections. At their best, reviews offer specific suggestions in a constructive environment that includes both compliments and criticism.

The proposal coordinator's role is to set the stage for the latter situation by:

- Allowing adequate time for thorough reviews

- Selecting the appropriate reviewers

- Setting the ground rules

- Pointing out what is helpful and what is damaging

- Providing detailed instructions to reviewers

- Facilitating the review to ensure that reviewers carry through with their mission.

## SCHEDULING REVIEWS

Three traditional proposal reviews are:

- *The storyboard review.* The storyboard review occurs early in the proposal process, when authors have completed a modified storyboard form, as illustrated in Sample A. The proposal team often holds this review without outside reviewers.

- *The Pink Team review.* The Pink Team review is another early review of the first fleshed-out version of the proposal. Some folks suggest that this review should be held when the proposal is 75 percent complete, but in my experience, the Pink Team Review copy of the proposal is more likely to be 25 to 50 percent complete. I think this might be more appropriate timing because some contributors lose track of their original ideas when moving from the storyboard to the Pink Team draft. It's better to redirect misguided contributors early in the process than to wait for the 75-percent completion point. The review team includes representative technical personnel and mid-level managers.

- *The Red Team review.* The Red Team review is normally the final review before the proposal moves into production. Reviewers tend to include senior-level managers, at least one of whom has the authority to commit on behalf of the company.

I know of no formula for scheduling reviews. I schedule them and all other aspects of the proposal by backing up from the date the proposal must be delivered. On the delivery end of the schedule, allow enough time to incorporate the Red Team comments and produce the proposal. On the kickoff end of the schedule, allow several days for start-up. Then spread the storyboard, Pink Team, and Red Team reviews over the remaining time, providing more days between the Pink Team and Red Team reviews than between the storyboard and Pink Team reviews.

## ALLOWING ADEQUATE TIME FOR THOROUGH REVIEWS

Beside the factors I discuss below, the most common problem with reviews is that they are not long enough. Reviewers need adequate time to read and digest the assigned materials before commenting on them; otherwise they tend to make on-the-fly comments. Such comments can be inconsequential, meaningful, or outright deadly. Providing adequate time to read and digest material tends to eliminate outright deadly comments. Let me provide an example.

I recently prepared a small proposal to process mapping imagery. The procedure for processing the images was partially computerized and partially manual, so that the image processing system, per se, consisted of machines and humans. Not having adequately digested the material they were reading and being from a corporate unit that was unaccustomed to partially manual systems, the Red Team reviewers strongly objected to any mention of humans in the proposal because they felt such mention pointed up an area of weakness.

A less experienced writer might have caved in at this point, since the reviewers included the president of the organization and several senior division managers. It was clear to me, however, that omitting mention of the human components of this system would result in a non-compliant proposal that told just half the story. I ignored the Red Team, explaining my actions to the capture manager and lead technical contributors. Reason prevailed.

Not all on-the-fly comments have the potential to wreak havoc on the subject proposal. Nevertheless, the best way to close the opening for ill-considered suggestions is to provide adequate time. To provide adequate time, you need the backing of your senior-level management Only they can make proposal reviews a priority, and only they can juggle assignments to free time and money for reviews and reviewers.

Enroll your managers in the review process by pointing out the cost-to-benefit ratio, and use that ratio as your own guide to the length of the review. The benefit of a thorough review, relative to the cost, grows in direct proportion to the size of the proposed contract. Although you may be willing to let a proposal for a small contract slide by with a mediocre review, the same does not apply to a proposal for a large or keystone contract.

Arrive at your own estimate of the number of pages that a reviewer should read, based on how your proposal is formatted and who is reviewing. I've seen one estimate that each reviewer should be assigned no more than 30 pages to review. This might be a reasonable rule of thumb.

## SELECTING THE APPROPRIATE REVIEWERS

The capture manager is normally responsible for selecting the proposal reviewers. The proposal coordinator should confirm with the capture manager the qualifications of each reviewer to make certain that all or most angles are covered, particularly for the Red Team. Reviewers should include the following:

- A representative who can commit on behalf of the company

- A representative from each major programmatic aspect of the solution being proposed—for example, networking, software development, and computer support; or medical and administrative

- A representative of the management team for the proposed contract *PROGRAM MGR*

- A compliance reviewer. *WHO FOCUSES ONLY ON THIS.*

A representative who can commit on behalf of the company will ensure that the company can deliver on all promises made in the proposal. Program and management representatives will check on their colleagues' work regarding the technical and management aspects of the proposal. The compliance reviewer's sole job is ensuring that all RFP requirements are addressed.

## SETTING THE GROUND RULES

A strange thing happens when people are given the opportunity to exercise power over other people: A few people will abuse their power. Interestingly, the abusers are most often not the senior-level managers who have learned how to coax and cajole their worker bees into producing day after day, but lower-level personnel who seem smitten by the opportunity to review the work of others and eager to demonstrate how much they know.

These people cause much of the damage done in reviews not by what they say but by *how* they say it. For this reason, it's important to establish ground rules that focus as much on tone of voice as content.

I advocate a review approach that employs direct communication in conjunction with practical people skills. I don't take this stand on moral grounds, that is, because I think people *should* be nice. Rather, I find it to be a pragmatic rule of thumb that leads to the results we're seeking—a winning proposal without stress.

Tone of voice can make the critical difference in whether or not a contributor actually hears and uses what is being said and written. Additionally, the tone of voice used during the review is often an important factor in defining the emotional environment for the remainder of the proposal process. Because you will have to live with the proposal team long after the reviewers have returned to their offices, it behooves the proposal coordinator to set ground rules that will make life easier rather than more difficult.

Setting the ground rules thus includes reminding reviewers to say what they have to say using their best Miss Manners tone of voice, preferably without sarcasm, direct personal insults, or too much attention to copyediting. This does not mean that reviewers have to compliment when compliments are unwarranted; it does imply that to leave the contributor with the psychological energy to continue, reviewers must make their points without turning egos into egg yolks. Healthy people of all ages—children and adults alike—produce better when you draw them out rather than kick them in the behind.

Remind reviewers that the best way to keep disdain from creeping into their voices is to consider that no matter what the reviewer learned from a mentor, a favorite consultant, or personal experience, no one has a monopoly on how to write proposals beyond making them compliant, and sometimes compliance is iffy, too. I happen to be a literal, step-by-step kind of person, so the guts of my proposals are linear in structure: First we do this, then we do that, and then we do another thing. Dum de dum de dum de dum. But I've seen writers who twist everything around—Dum dum de de de de de—to make a marketing point, and win! Some reviewers like vanilla, some like chocolate, and a few oddballs like strawberry.

Which brings me to a point about the proposal coordinator's role. If you're paying attention, you should know what is wrong and right with a proposal before it goes into a review. Being aware, you should head off devastating reviews by working with the capture manager to get the support needed before a major review takes place.

## POINTING OUT WHAT IS HELPFUL AND WHAT IS NOT

My guidelines for proposal reviewers are designed to remind people of what they already know: Anyone can accept and even welcome criticism if it is presented in a manner that is not intimidating. I suggest that you prepare slides or written instructions for the review team listing the following pertinent points. Expand upon them before the review begins.

- *Bite your tongue.* Certain comments are forbidden. Remarks like "They're clearly asking for . . ." or "This section misses the point entirely" are unacceptable. No rolling your eyes to the tune of "Just Answer the Mail." Make certain your tone of voice conveys the fact that you understand the ramifications of what you are saying or make that fact known directly with words such as, "I understand the effort you've put into the technical volume and the additional effort that will be needed to change it. . . ."

- *Refrain from sharing negative interpretations, unless they are critical to an argument for or against a particular tack.* By emphasizing what is needed rather than what is wrong with the section, one can automatically avoid interjecting negative interpretations like "this section strikes me as bull. . ." or "this section sounds apologetic." "I think we need to replace some of this material with hard facts" or "I think we must be more aggressive here" are more positive interpretations that make the same point. Follow up with examples of the hard facts or the aggressive statements that could be used.

In marking up a document, comments like "this is arrogant" or "this word is obtuse" are simply not helpful. If the writer agreed with you, he or she wouldn't have used that word in the first place, and—believe it or not—your comments are again almost always a matter of interpretation rather than fact. (I'm ashamed to admit it, but I've been known to look up words after the Red Team just to see if they implied something of which I was unaware. In every instance, the reviewer's interpretation was absent from the dictionary definition of the word. The interpretation was personal and subjective.) Simply cross out the word and replace it with the one of your choice. If you must, make a note saying, "This word would work better here." If you want to be more forceful, write, "Replace this word with. . . ."

- *Own your comments.* Use "I think this needs. . ." rather than "This needs. . . ." By using the term "I," you remind yourself and the section author that you are stating one person's opinion, not a fact. Note that using the term "we" when describing what must be done to improve the section also serves as a reminder to the reviewer and to the writer that they belong to one team—the winning team.

- *Be specific and thorough.* Instead of writing two words as a reminder, write a whole sentence. This will invariably save the writer from playing phone tag to find out what you meant.

- *For big problems, coordinate your response.* Let's say the proposal has *big* problems—so big that entire sections must be trashed. Seek agreement from other reviewers and select a spokesperson who says, "We've come to the conclusion that this proposal must be rewritten for this, this, this, and this reason," without making anyone look like a doofus for not seeing it from your perspective in the first place.

Remember that if something is terribly awry with your proposal or a piece of it, those who created the mess may be unable to fix it. Some writers are not switch hitters. They are unable to go from vanilla to chocolate to strawberry and back again. Sometimes this is because the writers haven't dissected their own writing style and played with the pieces to see other ways they can put them back together. Howard Gardner's *Frames of Mind*, another book that offers insight to writers of every ilk, explains various kinds of intelligence, revealing why some technical geniuses are incapable of putting their thoughts into coherent sentences, let alone changing those sentences so that others like them.

If extra troops are needed, high-level reviewers should arrange for added assistance or replace one team with another, but they should never, ever,

*ever* promise something that they can't produce. And they shouldn't bother hammering heads about what went wrong in the meantime.

Encourage frequent reviewers to develop analytical and instructional skills so that they can explain clearly to writers where they've gone astray and what to do to correct the problem. Ask them to pose the question, "What is wrong with this section, and what are the top three suggestions I can make to set it right?" Remember that when preparing proposals, people usually go with their instincts. If instincts have led a contributor astray, generalities won't get him back on track. He needs specific pointers in the right direction.

## REVIEWING RÉSUMÉS

To paraphrase Robert Frost, something there is that doesn't love a résumé. People loathe reviewing them. Besides, if résumés are part of a larger review, they often seem to be addenda to, rather than part of, the meat of the proposal. If résumés will carry significant weight during the government evaluation, it makes good sense to hold a separate résumé review using individuals who serve as the in-line supervisors to the people proposed.

For the best résumé review I've ever seen, we asked five managers being proposed for a new contract to review the résumés of those proposed to work for them. As the day-to-day supervisors of those same personnel, the managers easily identified gaps in the relevant experience and overblown statements of competence. They were able to add, delete, and correct information by calling the individuals with questionable credentials and resolving issues on the spot.

I have no doubt that such reviews contribute greatly to a winning proposal.

## HOLDING A WALL REVIEW

In Chapter 8, I describe two types of storyboards: the classic and the modified. Classic storyboards evolve on the wall and are traditionally reviewed in what I call a wall review. The modified storyboard is reviewed on the wall or in a paper review.

An advantage of a wall review is that all the comments end up on the wall itself or in the author's notebook. If suggestions are contradictory, the contradiction can be resolved in an immediate exchange among all reviewers. This is easier than collecting numerous sets of comments and scheduling separate meetings to resolve the contradictions that inevitably arise. Given these advantages, one would be foolish not to hold a wall review when possible.

For a wall review in today's environment, distribute copies of the RFP, storyboards, and instructions to all reviewers, asking reviewers to read all storyboards ahead of time. A sample set of instructions to reviewers is provided in Sample F.

Name a facilitator, possibly yourself or the capture manager, who has the ability to guide the tone and content of the meeting. The facilitator should make himself familiar with the content of the proposal to the extent that he can guide the discussions and resolve differences. Follow these additional steps:

- *Set up a schedule for the facilitator that will allow the team to review all storyboards within the allotted time, with regular breaks.* If your final proposal will be 100 to 150 pages, you can probably review all storyboards in one day. If not, schedule accordingly. Schedule short restroom breaks every hour.

- *Appoint a timer to assist in keeping the facilitator and team on schedule.*

- *Set up tables so that all reviewers and teammates can see the storyboards, although they will not be able to read them.*

- *Contract for a caterer to provide lunch in the conference room with beverages, plates, napkins, and utensils.* Stock the room with additional coffee and sodas and perhaps light snacks, such as granola bars.

- *Equip the room with a whiteboard or slide projector with blank transparencies—something that the team can use to illustrate points, if necessary.* Provide the necessary accessories, such as markers and erasers.

- *Copy extra sets of the RFP and storyboards for the forgetful.*

- *Appoint a compliance reviewer.* This reviewer's only job is to review the storyboards for compliance with Sections C, L, and M. The compliance reviewer should perform his work before the wall review but should attend the review to present comments.

At the appointed time, convene the reviewers in the storyboard room with all the proposal team members and follow these steps:

- *Introduce any reviewers who are not members of the design team, and introduce the design team to reviewers.* Provide a name and a few sentences indicating why the reviewers were selected and to whom sections were assigned. "Joe manages our contract with the FHA, which is very similar to the contract we're proposing here," "Jane is the lead networking engineer at the FAA," or "Tim is in charge of the management piece."

- *Review the schedule for the day and state goals.* "We will be walking through the storyboards one by one, using Jim as the facilitator and Nancy as the timer. The individuals responsible for each of the storyboards will take notes as we review their storyboards. By lunch, we should have completed Section 4. By 5:00, we should have arrived at the final storyboard. We have allocated one-half hour for lunch, and we've scheduled short breaks every hour so that you can move around. If you find yourself getting groggy, feel free to stand or pace in the back of the room. Our goal for the day will be to have reviewed all storyboards and resolved all issues related to the review. The whiteboard (or projector) is here for that purpose."

- *Remind reviewers of the instructions provided to them, including how to be constructive, rather than destructive, in making their remarks and suggestions.*

- *Ask the facilitator to take over, the timer to begin timing, and the first section contributor to begin taking notes.*

Although each person should have a copy of the storyboards in hand, the facilitator works from the wall to focus attention there. She can employ brainstorming to come up with additional information for weak sections and move to the whiteboard or projector to work out contradictory comments.

At the end of the review, ask reviewers if they have communicated all their comments to the facilitator. If not, collect marked-up copies. Then separate the marked copies by section and distribute them to the responsible contributors. If section breaks overlap, you will need to copy overlapping pages (only if they are marked with comments) so that each writer gets a full set of comments.

## HOLDING A PINK TEAM OR RED TEAM REVIEW

The structures of Pink and Red Teams are the same:

- *A review team convenes in a conference room.*

- *A facilitator instructs the reviewers and assigns sections for reading and reviewing.* If the proposal is short, each reviewer might read the entire proposal. If the proposal is large, reviewers are usually assigned pieces of the proposal for reading. Sometimes reviewers are asked to score the proposal using a formula.

- *When reviewers have completed their sections, the team regroups and prepares briefing slides for the proposal team.* The slides cover major points and present the results of any section scoring.

- *The proposal team is invited to hear the reviewers' comments.* The review team makes a presentation to the proposal team and answers questions.

Although this scheme works to a certain extent, it has flaws. First, most people feel uneasy in a quiet room with lots of other people. If you have the space, I recommend sending people off to offices after they have received their instructions. If each reviewer can be placed in a colleague's office, where answering the phone or playing with the computer is less tempting than it is in one's own office, so much the better.

Second, because most reviews for most proposals last one day, reviewers often present their comments to the team in the evening, when most people are at their worst. Because the proposal team and reviewers are anxious to get home, they tend to refrain from challenging reviewers and don't ask appropriate questions. I don't have a solution for this problem other than reconvening the next day, if possible. In reality, part of the review team has usually flown away by that time.

For my ideal review, I would disseminate the review package with instructions, ask reviewers to read the proposal independently, and convene the group only after all reviewers have finished their reading and marking. Unfortunately, experience says it will never happen.

Planning for the Pink or Red Team review is much like planning for the storyboard review:

- *Select reviewers whose talents and experience match those being proposed.* Ideally, you should retain two reviewers for each major subject area:

networking, software development, help desk support, etc. A double review protects against over-criticism on the part of a reviewer who disagrees with the style employed or strategy taken by a particular author. Also, more ideas are always better.

- *Appoint a compliance reviewer.* This reviewer's only job is to review the proposal for compliance with Sections C, L, and M.

- *Name a facilitator to guide the tone and content of the meeting.* Again, this reviewer should at least skim the entire proposal and must be able to guide reviewers to a satisfactory conclusion.

- *If the proposal is large, break it into logical pieces and make assignments based on subject matter expertise.* Estimate the time needed to review each section.

- *Set up a schedule that will allow the team to review all the sections within the allotted time, with regular breaks.* If this proposal is a "must win," make sure that your managers are not skimping on the review process. Give the review all the people and time it needs.

- *If reading will be done in a conference room, reserve the largest room available.* Consider renting a room in a nearby hotel if your own facilities are inadequate.

- *Arrange seating for individual reading and for presentations, avoiding the single, oval conference table if you can.* If the room is large enough, you can set up tables facing a whiteboard or projection screen *and* individual seating. For reading, arrange reviewers so that they are not directly across from each another. If a single conference table is all you have, try to seat people in every other or every third seat to allow elbow room.

- *Contract with a caterer to provide lunch in the conference room with beverages, plates, napkins, and utensils.* Stock the room with additional coffee and sodas for all tastes and light snacks.

- *Equip the room with a whiteboard or slide projector with blank transparencies*—something that the team can use to illustrate points, if necessary. Provide the necessary accessories, such as markers and erasers.

- *Copy one RFP, compliance matrix, and proposal for each reviewer.* Put the RFP and the proposal in three-ring binders.

- *Copy review forms if you are planning to use them.* Sample E is an example.

- *Send each reviewer a notice of the date, time, and length of the review, based on your projections.* Suggest that reviewers wear casual, comfortable clothes.

On the review day, convene the reviewers in the review room and follow these steps:

- *Introduce the reviewers.* Provide a name and a few sentences indicating why the reviewers were selected.

- *Outline the schedule for the day.*

- *Provide the reviewers with instructions and associated forms.* Sample slides for instructing Pink and Red teams are found in Chapter 4.

- *If you use a rating scheme, explain how the scheme is to be applied.* Chapter 4 also contains example slides showing a rating scheme that can be used in conjunction with the Section M evaluation factors and instructions for its use.

- *Ask reviewers to remove compliance matrices from the front of the review package so they can be used freely.*

- *Ask reviewers to refrain from copyediting.* Some people are incapable of doing this—me included—but formatting and checking for grammar and spelling should be way, way down on the reviewers' list of priorities.

- *Ask for questions and comments, make sure that all reviewers have the required documents, and let the races begin.*

Throughout the review process, the facilitator answers questions, checks progress, and assists the section assignees in completing the review process, if asked.

## CONSOLIDATING THE REVIEW COMMENTS

When the reviewers have completed rating their sections, the entire review team is reconvened to exchange information. I recommend using an oral process of reporting and reconciling ratings. The oral process is particularly important because proposal sections are often structured in parallel to complement each other and to reflect organizational consistency. If such sections are assigned to different reviewers and one reviewer suggests structural changes while another does not, these inconsistencies become

TECH + MGMT. VOLUMES
REFLECT COMMON THEMES

evident in the oral report. Reviewers can then reconcile them immediately with the help of the facilitator. This is a good reason to use a facilitator who is intimately familiar with the proposal so that she can pick up on problems if the reviewers don't recognize them on their own.

*If all reviewers read all sections of the proposal,* the facilitator's job is to distill a single rating for each section and arrive at three primary methods to improve the section from all the reviewer comments. This is best done in a committee formed from the entire group, so that all issues can be resolved as a team. The facilitator takes the following steps to create a draft slide, section by section:

- Asks each reviewer for his rating of the section

- Asks each reviewer for his top three suggestions for improvements

- Asks each reviewer for other suggestions

- Asks each reviewer for resource needs.

The facilitator writes all the responses on the whiteboard, resolving discrepancies one by one. Only after the team has agreed on the answer to one question does the facilitator move on to the next.

If time is an issue, the facilitator can divide the reviewers into small groups and assign each group to a section, providing that group with all the ratings for the assigned section. Each group then prepares a *draft* slide in the same manner as described above. Major discrepancies are brought back to the team and resolved with all present following these steps:

- *The facilitator returns section rating sheets to their owners.* The reviewers can then compare their comments to those on the draft slide.

- *A representative of each group presents the draft slide.*

- *The facilitator resolves any differences that arise when reviewers compare their comments to the synthesized slide.*

If the sections were separated for review, the facilitator asks a representative of each section to present the major findings as they appear on the rating sheet. This is an oral presentation, so all reviewers hear all comments. If everyone is tuned in, the presentation offers the opportunity to reconcile contradictions and present consistent information *across all sections.*

## PREPARING SLIDES

When all discrepancies are resolved, the facilitator prepares slides, showing the rating, three major points for each section, other suggestions, and needed resources, as shown in Example 9-1. These slides are usually handwritten, but with newer technologies, your corporation may have the capability to create formal slides quickly.

**Example 9-1:** Example Debriefing Slide

### Section 5

- **Rating**: Blue

- **Three Suggestions for Improvement**:
  —Add two subsections entitled:
    1) Maintenance of networked systems, and
    2) Troubleshooting networked systems
  —Reverse the first two subsections to be compliant with Section C.
  —Rewrite section on designing networked systems

- **Also**: Rework theme sentences and action captions per markup

- **Resources**: For rewriting networked systems, Don Wilson

Select a presenter for each slide. This should be one of the reviewers who reviewed the pertinent section.

## HOLDING A RED TEAM DEBRIEFING

When all the debriefing slides have been prepared, invite the proposal team to join the reviewers:

- *Introduce the reviewers and the proposal team.*

- *Pass around a sign-in sheet with the names, phone numbers, and e-mail addresses of all reviewers and proposal team members.* During the debriefing, copy this sign-in sheet to distribute to all team members.

- *Explain that you will be walking through the slides using a section reviewer as presenter.*

- *Ask the proposal team to hold comments and questions until the presenter has completed his commentary on the slide.*

- *If significant issues arise during the debriefing, the facilitator mediates.*

- *If issues cannot be resolved on the spot, the facilitator identifies individuals who will participate in resolving them, setting meeting times for those individuals and deadlines for resolution.*

- *The facilitator also designates an individual to secure the resources that the review team has suggested, either by section or for all sections.*

- *At the close of the debriefing, the facilitator reads back all the commitments made.*

- *Distribute the sign-in sheet to the reviewers.* Ask reviewers and the proposal team to call or e-mail the appropriate person if they have delayed reactions or suddenly come up with just the right fix for a problem section.

- *Gather mark-ups and rating sheets from the reviewers.*

- *Thank the reviewers graciously and send them home.*

- *With the proposal team, schedule a meeting early the next day to plan your recovery.*

## DISTRIBUTING THE REVIEW COMMENTS

Take these steps to distribute the review comments:

- *Split the marked-up proposals and the rating sheets by section.* If all reviewers read all sections, you will have numerous markups and rating sheets for each section. If only two reviewers read each section, you will have two proposal markups and one rating sheet for each section.

- *Make one copy of the slides, markups, and rating sheets.* This is a tad neurotic, but you don't want to take a chance of losing these suggestions if something should happen to one of your proposal team members.

- *Distribute sets of the slides, markups, and rating sheets to the section authors.* You can omit the rating sheets and simply distribute the markups and slides if all pertinent comments have been included on the final slides. However, sometimes the reviewer rating sheets hold valuable side comments that were dropped from the final slide presentation.

## INCORPORATING REVIEW COMMENTS

Usually, section authors are responsible for incorporating review comments, following the storyboard and Pink Team reviews. Consequently, all the design team members are clear on their instructions. After storyboard or Pink Team reviews, you might not need to hold a follow-up meeting.

Follow-up after the Red Team review should be more structured because comments have originated from higher-level reviewers, and the production deadline looms in the near future. I recommend holding a follow-up meeting to resolve any outstanding issues and to prepare a schedule for completing the required changes to meet the production deadline.

Providing a literal outline of all Red Team changes is impractical, but outlining major changes or changes that must be made to all sections is a possibility. I have sometimes prepared tables like the one shown in Example 9-2 for this purpose.

**Example 9-2:** Example Red Team Follow-up Table

| Change | Person | Date |
|---|---|---|
| Remove Dan Howard; replace with Lisa Riley (management section) | Janet | 11/22 |
| Remove Dan Howard; replace with Lisa Riley (résumé) | Michael | 11/24 |
| Rewrite second half of executive summary | Jamie | 11/27 |
| Reformat Figure 2-9 | Angela | 11/25 |

## FORESEEING THE FUTURE OF PROPOSAL REVIEWS

Groupware, as it is used in business process reengineering, allows teams of people working from laptop computers to make decisions collectively on a network. I foresee a time when rating sheets will be on a local area network and facilitators will be able to compile information by clicking on an icon. The Internet holds similar possibilities.

Be aware, however, of what editors have long realized and the military tested many years ago when developing computer screens: People overlook onscreen what they would catch on paper. The advantage of paper is that you can hold two pages in front of you at the same time, comparing one to the other. On most current screens, this is not easily done, and the reader often loses the larger context of the section he is reviewing. He can't remember whether a certain point has been made or not and may inadvertently interject points that have been made on the previous page or delete a point that he feels should be made elsewhere, forgetting then to insert it at the better location.

This can also occur using hard copy, but it's easier to remedy the problem on hard copy for the reasons mentioned above: It's easier to compare pages on hard copy than on the screen.

If you're going to use online reviews, make certain that—at a minimum—you turn on tracking mechanisms so that any change the reviewer makes is marked. The proposal coordinator can then accept or decline the changes individually.

# CHAPTER 10

# *Producing the Proposal*

The production process includes any activities that staff members perform to piece the proposal together and spruce it up, including moving text from one software program to another, placing or pasting up graphics, copyediting, creating front matter and collateral material, reproducing, and assembling the whole shebang in three-ring binders with covers, spines, and tabs. The production process can also include creating a soft copy of the proposal for delivery with the hard copy.

This is detail work that really belongs to a production manager but is often assigned in smaller companies to the proposal coordinator. Whether you handle it yourself or coordinate with a production manager, it is in the proposal coordinator's best interests to know what must be done, how it is done, and the time frame for doing it. This is a self-defensive step for preventing the stress of late-arriving binders, misproportioned covers, and schedules based on delusion. Remember, the commitment is to a winning proposal without stress.

The specifics of producing a final proposal are ultimately dependent upon the software systems used and the staff available for production. In this chapter, I address the aspects of review and final production that are not specific to certain software, conveying a general sense of what the proposal coordinator does at each step.

## THINKING ABOUT PRODUCTION

To schedule the elements of production accurately, the proposal coordinator must first inspect Section L for requirements that will have ramifications during production. Does Section L specify:

1. *How the proposal is to be paginated (within each section vs. straight through the document)?* If the proposal must be paginated straight through, none of the sections within a volume can be printed for the final document until the sections preceding it are printed. Particularly if you have very large volumes, schedule sections for production sequentially, or you will find yourself bumping into a deadline.

2. *How many pages the proposal will have?* This writer's nightmare is a production boon, in that you know the ultimate size of the proposal and you can safely order binders, covers, spines, and paper.

3. *How large figures are to be presented (construction proposals often include enormous schedules that are submitted in cardboard tubes)?* Plan for the services and products needed to develop and present over-sized graphics.

4. *That the proposal must be submitted in soft-copy format, and if so, in what format (Word for Windows, WordPerfect)?* If you must submit the proposal on diskette, your production process might be slightly longer, particularly if you must convert from one software program to another. Importantly, you must make sure that you have the software capability to convert from one application to another and to write to diskettes in the required format.

5. *That your company must provide any other soft-copy items, such as sample products or demonstration programs?* If so, how many diskettes must be provided with the original version of the proposal and with each copy? Consider ordering clear plastic diskette holders, which hold four 3.5-inch diskettes and are punched for three-hole binders.

6. *That you must include glossy brochures, user manuals, specification sheets, or similar material on the products you are proposing?* If so, how many? Consider how these items will be included. Can they be hole-punched and placed in a three-ring binder? Will you slip them into plastic sleeves designed for three-ring binders? Will you provide one set of originals and "n" sets of copies?

   As I've mentioned before, I have participated in producing proposals that ultimately included 17 volumes of support documents and product specifications. Reproducing these documents—which were bound in various ways and had to be unbound—was an overwhelming reproduction effort that had to be exquisitely organized, because products and accompanying documentation were changing right down to the deadline. Plan and act accordingly.

7. *That you must prepare elements of your proposal for a stand-up presentation rather than a printed document?* Consider the production requirements for preparing color slides or transparencies and collecting or creating collateral material, such as charts and graphs.

8. *That you must provide a sanitized copy of the cost proposal?* Locating someone who is allowed access to pricing information and who will take the time to do the tedious work of taping or whiting-out price information can be difficult, but it is sometimes required.

Section C and other relevant specifications are important parts of the equation. The length of Section C can dictate the length of the proposal in bids where you are required to provide a one-to-one correlation between Section C and one or more parts of the proposal. The length of the proposal, in combination with the number of copies required, in turn dictates the time needed for copying.

Once you have researched the government's requirements and their ramifications, assess the elements of your proposal by asking the following questions:

1. *Are you using any or many 11 x 17-inch or similar foldouts?* If so, plan how will you be placing the titles and page numbers on these foldouts. Will you be typing them in a separate file and physically pasting them up? Will the graphic artist be typing the title into the graphics file?

   Do you have an in-house capability to reproduce 11 x 17-inch pages? Will you be folding these large pages by hand or, instead, handing this terribly boring process over to a professional print shop?

2. *Are you including by choice any unwieldy documents, such as appendices or support material, as addressed in item 6 above?* How will you present them?

3. *Are you including any other items that require special production, handling, or packaging?*

4. *How will you be packing the proposal?* Do you need to order boxes, tape, and labels?

Use this information to create a schedule that looks like Example 10-1.

You would do well to overlay this schedule on the writing and review schedule to remind yourself when production issues should be handled or when to touch base with the production manager. Adjust the schedule if milestones change as you move toward final production.

**Example 10-1:** Sample Production Schedule

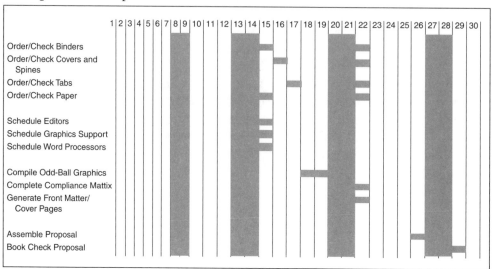

## PRODUCING REVIEW DRAFTS

The first step in producing a review draft is defining a drop-dead date and time for authors to submit proposal text and graphics. Leave time for printing, assembling, copying, and preparing review books. Judge the time needed by assessing the in-house or outside copying resources, the number of review books needed, and the help available to prepare them. You may need only half a day to produce the Pink Team review book and a full day to produce the Red Team book.

For a storyboard or Pink Team review, compile a printout of these materials:

- The compliance matrix

- All text sections

- All graphics

- The executive summary, if it is available.

For the Red Team, expand this list to include the following items:

- An inside cover page with the requisite nondisclosure statement

- A draft table of contents without page numbers

- A draft list of figures without page numbers

- Appendices

- Résumés

- Acronym list

- Cover pages for appendices, résumés, the Acronym List, etc.

Follow these steps to produce your finished review document:

1. *Assemble the front matter and text sections as they will appear in the final document.*

2. *Assemble the graphics printouts sequentially by tracking number.*

3. *Reduce fold-out graphics to 8.5 x 11 on the copier, as long as they remain legible after reduction.*

4. *Section by section, insert the graphics by matching the tracking number in the text file with the tracking number of the graphic printout.* Place the graphic printout behind the page where the figure or table will finally appear.

5. *Copy the entire set on three-hole-punch paper.* Make a set for each member of the proposal team and the review team, with a few extras for emergencies. Or, if you are dividing volumes among reviewers, copy only the appropriate volume for each reviewer. (If your reviewers will be reading only specific sections of a volume, I suggest you provide them with the entire volume so they can get a sense of the scope of the proposal and have an opportunity to check other sections for duplicate or missing information if issues arise.)

6. *Insert colored slip sheets between sections if you see an advantage in doing so.* You can also use colored tabs.

7. *Place each review copy in a three-ring binder, with the compliance matrix on top.* You will be suggesting that reviewers remove the matrix so that they don't have to flip back and forth to use it as a reference. If you provide an acronym list that is not required as an appendix, slip it into the inside front pouch of the binder.

8. *If you have a draft copy of the proposal cover, insert it into the see-through cover pouch on the review binders.*

Some proposal coordinators place graphics into the text file for the Red Team review. This makes for a better-looking document, but, as they say in the technology business, it is a non-trivial activity. Placing and sizing the graphics and then adjusting the layout is very time-consuming. For a large proposal, these steps can take several days. This step is best left for final production, particularly if your writers will be returning to online work after the Red Team.

For reviews, I even tend to be a bit sloppy with other elements of the layout, such as tables that run from one page to the next and headings that are orphaned at the bottom of a page. In my experience, perfectionist tendencies applied at this time make little difference in the ultimate review results.

Save binders and tabs for the next review.

## PACKAGING THE PROPOSAL

Most proposals are provided to the government in the form of an original and a designated number of copies. The original of the first volume and the cost proposal normally contain copies of the transmittal letter (and any other documents requiring a signature) with an original signature. If the proposal must be provided in soft-copy format, the diskettes are also included with the original of the first volume or the cost volume.

Proposals are most often packaged in three-ring binders with see-through pockets on the outside and opaque pockets on the inside. The see-through pockets house the front and back covers and the spine. The opaque pocket in the front can be used for an acronym list, the transmittal letter, or glossy marketing materials, as you choose. Numbered or named tabs separate major sections or groups of sections, as you choose or as the government specifies. Some executive summaries are to be provided as a separate document and can end up as staple-bound, glossy marketing materials.

The proposal coordinator produces the proposal for reviews and delivery. She makes decisions affecting production, however, throughout the proposal process. The fancier the proposal, the more attention the proposal coordinator must pay to creating covers and spines; producing fold-out pages, the executive summary, and tabs; and selecting products and vendors along the way.

**Producing Cover, Spines, and Tabs**

Companies vary greatly in their ability to produce covers, spines, and tabs internally. If you use outside vendors or rely on a different division of your company to produce these parts of the proposal, begin working with them early in the proposal process to agree on what will be produced and when. If you have a short proposal schedule—say, 30 days—do not hesitate to get these things started.

Even if a production manager is handling these aspects of the proposal, the proposal coordinator should understand the processes and consider the following facts when deciding what the covers, spines, and tabs should look like and how they will be produced. Keep these guidelines in mind:

- *The bigger the binder, the larger the cover.* So I'm stupid, but it took me several proposals to figure out that larger binders have larger cover dimensions. I guess I thought that the spine grew but the covers were fixed, as is the case with bound books. This is not so of binders. While the top-to-bottom measurement is stable as a family of binders grows, the left-to-right dimension gets larger.

- *To order binders, you need to know the number of pages in each volume.* If you want your covers and spines to fit snugly into the binder, you need to know (or estimate) in advance the final size of each of your proposal volumes. Then you need to measure a sample binder to identify the inside dimensions of the cover pouch. Sometimes this is impossible, so proposal coordinators don't even attempt to make appropriately sized covers and spines.

- *Covers and spines look better when they are sized to fit the binder.* Since this fact is a third corollary to the statements made above, I've figured out a way to design round the uncertainty. Ask the artist to design a cover graphic to the size of the smallest possible cover that you think could be used *and* to design it so that you can include a border that will fill in the remaining space if you end up using a larger binder, as Example 10-2 illustrates.

**Example 10-2:** Sample Cover Sized to Fit Binder Using Extendable Borders

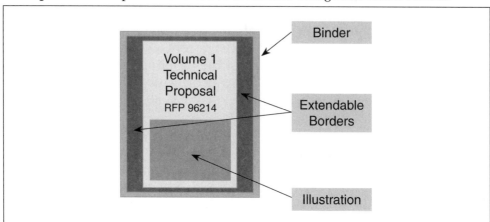

This is not a simple matter of shrinking or enlarging the cover graphic, because the top-to-bottom dimension of the binder does not change; only the side-to-side measurement gets bigger. Consequently, the border on the final graphic may be larger on the sides than it is on the top and bottom. This is an imperfect solution, but it works for an imperfect world in which you can't hold up work on your cover art until you know with certainty the final binder size.

- *To produce a graphic that is wider than 8.5 x 11, you need special print capabilities.* When my resources have been limited, I've printed out a cover and spines on plain 8.5 x 11 paper and pasted them up to make an odd-sized camera-ready cover. Then I've asked a vendor to copy the cover onto large-size cover stock. Some venders have this capability and others don't, so check before counting on this option.

- *To avoid paste-up for high-quality graphics, you need a high-end printer.* High-end printers can produce grayscales for copying or film for color separations in various sizes. A handful of companies have such printer capabilities in-house, but most use pre-print service organizations or full-service print houses to provide these products. If you don't have a full-time production manager, confer with your artist about your graphics software and your system capabilities to plan in advance for a high-quality cover and spines. Then check with vendors to ascertain their capabilities.

- *Make test copies.* If you're planning to copy a color printout rather than printing it to create your covers, make a test copy on the final paper stock to make sure that you like the result.

- *Have vendors cut covers and spines.* I have hand-cut covers and spines in my time, but the results are uneven unless you're highly skilled with a cutting board. A vendor or an in-house production department can do a far better job.

- *Order printed tabs.* Professionally printed tabs make for a more formal proposal at a relatively low price. Order these as soon as your section headings are fixed, and check the proof sheets that the vendor provides carefully before you give the go-ahead for printing.

Tabs are printed in "banks," as illustrated in Example 10-3. The more tabs in a bank, the less space available for printing information on the tabs. Ideally, you want to use entire banks of tabs. For example, if you have ten sections in a volume, you would order two banks of five tabs. If you have six sections, you would order one bank of six tabs. If you have eight sections, you would order two banks of four tabs each.

**Example 10-3:** Sample Bank of Five Tabs

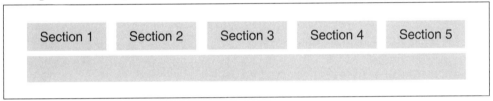

## Ordering Binders and Paper

I'm all for making a proposal look good in small, inexpensive ways. One of these is using colored binders and off-white paper. Gray is my favorite binder color. Gray gives the proposal that Brooks Brothers look without adding substantial cost. A cream-colored paper also cuts down on glare while adding a touch of class.

At the beginning of the proposal process, call vendors to see what they normally have in stock, and alert them to the fact that you will be ordering later. Put the paperwork, such as purchase orders, into the pipeline so you will have the binders and paper delivered when you want them.

## Copyediting the Final Proposal

By the time your proposal goes into final production, the proposal coordinator and the authors have read it numerous times, becoming blind to errors that copyeditors can quickly spot. For this reason I adamantly recommend production systems that include a copyediting cycle. Copyeditors can find ways to improve even near-perfect sentences, but their greater role is in catching items that the proposal coordinator or writers have grown sick of looking for, such as:

- *Typos and errors in usage that the spell checker can't detect* (from for form, if for it, it's for its)

- *Stylistic inconsistencies in product names* (Pagemaker vs. PageMaker, MS Word vs. Microsoft Word)

- *Lack of parallelism in lists* (create a slide, present a slide, and accepting questions from the audience)

- *Formatting inconsistencies in labels within graphics* (MONITOR, Hard Drive, keyboard)

- *Formatting inconsistencies in figure titles, table titles, and action captions* (Figure 1-2: The Keyboard Layout. vs. **Figure 1-3**. Our Network Design Methodology)

Even if you don't have a trained copyeditor on staff, get someone who has had no exposure to the proposal to read it. It will make you sleep better, and you won't be afraid to read the darn thing once it's out the door for fear that you will embarrass yourself by finding an egregious error.

The best time for copyediting is after the graphics have been placed. Copyediting and graphics placement can take place concurrently, however, if the copyeditor edits a printout of the graphics while the graphics are being placed, saving the text for later. Inevitably, some of the graphics will have to be replaced after corrections have been made. With most software, however, this becomes a relatively simple task once the graphics have been sized and the surrounding text has been formatted to fit the sizing. There is a tradeoff to everything.

### Flowing the Text and Placing the Graphics

Text is moved from word processing programs to desktop publishing programs by a process of "flowing" or "placing." The program operator then "places" or "inserts" the graphic at a point following its callout in the text. This is a process of matching the graphic tracking number in the text with the graphic tracking number of a graphic file and pulling that graphic file into the text file, as close as possible to the callout. Once the graphic is in the text file it usually must be sized by shrinking. The operator then adjusts the surrounding text so that paragraphs aren't broken when they don't need to be.

Even if your staff works in a word processing program, the process of tweaking here and there is grueling. It is made especially difficult when several figures or tables occur in close sequence, when numerous tables must be split over pages, or when a graphic suddenly turns out to be larger than the operator predicted.

If each section of the proposal begins at the top of the page, graphics can be placed section by section, beginning on the first page of the section and moving to the last. If sections begin at various points on the page, as is often true with page-limited proposals, graphic placement must begin on the first page of the first section and move through to the last page of the last section.

Of all the steps in the proposal process, this is the one that most consistently overruns its allotted time. Flowing the text into a desktop publishing package (if you are using one) and placing the graphics can cause personnel to stay at the office overnight and to push the panic button. For this reason, it is best to schedule a long lead time for final formatting or, if authors are overrunning their deadlines, begin final formatting while the authors are poking along on their last changes.

Remember, the commitment is to a winning proposal without stress, and placing graphics has bona fide potential for creating big stress. Juggle the schedule so that you move sections that are closest to completion into the production pipeline first. You can do this if your sections all begin at the top of a page, which is one very good reason to begin sections at the top of the page if you have the option.

If your sections run together over page breaks and the early sections are behind schedule, complete anything that you can while waiting, including those items addressed below: the table of contents, the compliance matrix, appendices, and the cover.

If it is feasible using your software, you can also save a small amount of time by dropping the graphics into their respective positions without adjusting the page layout while you're in waiting mode. Every little bit counts.

## Creating the Front Matter

The front matter of a proposal often includes the inside cover page, the table of contents, the list of figures, the compliance matrix, and the acronym list. These can also be stress producers if you leave them to the end of the proposal.

As discussed in Chapter 7, I always create a compliance and assignment matrix at the beginning of the proposal, update it as the proposal evolves, and delete the assignment columns when they are no longer needed. Unless the government dictates a strange format for the compliance matrix—such as identifying a page number for each Section C requirement—it is ready for production.

I also create the table of contents, the acronym list, cover pages for appendices, and the appendices themselves for the Red Team review so that they are already in place when the proposal goes into production. The last step in creating the printed document is assigning page numbers to each section in the table of contents and list of figures.

Because I like to be prepared, I shy away from using some of the automated tools for creating tables of contents and acronym lists. Automated systems allow the user to identify words or paragraphs that are eventually copied from the text files and plopped into a separate file. I don't want to have to pull these things together only after all the sections have been turned in for a review or the final production. I also find that in a distributed work environment where writers often perform some aspect of formatting the text, they are unreliable in assigning the appropriate styles. As a result, the software misses some headings and picks up a few words that are out of place.

If you are using a software program to create front matter, check the results by walking through the proposal page by page, comparing the headings, figures, or tables with those in the front matter. This goes quickly if you do it with another person.

## Writing a Transmittal Letter

Usually, a president or vice president of a company signs the transmittal letter, but because these individuals are sometimes too distracted to write one, the proposal coordinator gets the job. A transmittal letter usually looks something like Example 10-4, although some are more or less formal.

**Example 10-4:** Example Transmittal Letter

---

Shannon Associates, Inc.
1650 Irving Street, N.W.
Washington, D. C. 20010
(202) 234-9585

Mr. Martin Goldsmith
Contracting Officer
Room 1225
1937 Chester Avenue
Philadelphia, PA 19905

RE: RFP 0008412

Dear Mr. Goldsmith:

With this letter, Shannon Associates submits our proposal for the Health Services Help Desk in response to RFP 0003412 and Amendments 1, 2, and 3.

Our company has long experience providing Help Desk support to commercial clients in the Philadelphia area. We feel that the expertise gained in the commercial sector has strong carry-over to your agency and hope to employ it on the Health Services Help Desk contract.

Our proposal team looks forward to answering any questions you may have during the review process.

Sincerely,

Rebecca L. Shannon

---

Note that the example letter acknowledges response to the RFP and all amendments. Sometimes the government requires such acknowledgment in another section of the proposal, but it doesn't hurt to do so in the transmittal letter, too. I've seen letters that summarize the major win themes or mention previous experience, but I tend to think short and sweet is best.

## Copying the Proposal

Once you have pieced each volume of your proposal together section by section, you are ready to copy it. Make sure your in-house copier is in good working order or turn quickly to an outside copy shop. You don't want the copier to be jamming pages in the feeder, thus destroying your original as well as your patience. Just thinking about it raises my blood pressure.

And, if you can help it, don't do what most copy shops do, which is to make a copy of the original and use the new copy as if it were the original. Unless your copier provides exceptional output, a third-generation copy is noticeably poorer than a second-generation copy. If your copier ruins a page beyond help, reprint it.

If you're using a vendor—which makes reprinting damaged materials highly impractical—let the manager know that you're expecting high-quality copies. If the vendor cannot provide a third-generation copy that looks just like a second-generation copy, the results will be unsatisfactory.

### Assembling the Proposal

While your proposal is being formatted or copied, assemble the binders, covers, and spines volume by volume, making sure that you match the covers with appropriately sized binders. When the copies are ready, follow these steps:

- Open the binders and line them up around a large table.

- Open the binder rings and place a set of tabs next to—not in—the bindings.

- Place the copies into the binders, inserting tabs between sections.

- Move around the table and repeat.

This, of course, is a team activity. The more the merrier.

### Book Checking and Delivering the Proposal

Many items come together at the end of the proposal process: binders with covers, spines, tabs, and paper; text with graphics; front matter with narrative with appendices; Volume I with Volume II with Volume III. If your process has worked, they all fall neatly in place, amazing even the most experienced proposal coordinators.

Sometimes the results are perfect. Occasionally, they are less than perfect. A tradition in the proposal business is to check each copy of each volume for poor quality copies and missing pieces. To do this, turn each page in each volume, checking page numbers to see that all of the pages are in sequential order and none is missing.

Some copy shops will be happy to assemble your entire proposal, particularly if they have created the covers, spines, and tabs. If that option is too expensive or you don't trust them with complex instructions, assemble the proposal as described below.

This is another tedious job for which company is nice. Grab people from the hallway and do it.

I have only mailed a proposal several times. Most proposals—and particularly the more important ones—are hand delivered, even if the delivery point is several hours away by plane. If you do mail the proposal, make sure that you do it early enough to recover if the package is lost. And always get a receipt from the government noting the time of delivery.

## Creating Proposal Change Pages

*Change pages* are substitute pages that the government issues with an amendment (as described in Chapter 12), that the offeror issues in response to an amendment, or that the offeror issues in response to clarification requests and deficiency reports.

Large numbers of proposal change pages are a production nightmare. For the biggest proposal effort I've participated in, we created several sets of change pages in response to several sets of CRs and DRs. Each was a different color, and our proposal ended up looking like a rainbow.

Some of the newer automated systems for producing proposals may offer easy ways to create change pages, but I haven't seen them in use yet. These are the rules:

1. *Mark changes as specified by the government.* The preferred method of marking is with a change bar in the right-hand column. Most word-processing programs have a revision feature that automatically marks any changes to a page as they are made, using a bar, underlining, strike-through, and color options.

2. *Replace each outdated page with a change page or pages.*

3. *If one old page is replaced with two or more new pages, mark every page after the first as a continuation page.* For example, the first change page is 298; the second change page is 298-A; the third is 298-B.

4. *Maintain unchanged pages.* All pages surrounding a changed page must remain stable. Text remains stable; page numbering remains stable.

5. *Color-code sets of change pages to identify visually where changes are made.* The government sometimes requires color coding and specifies the color to be used with each set of changes.

This is how you make change pages on the computer:

1. *Create a directory labeled "Change."* Make a copy of your original proposal, and put it in the Change directory. I'll call this your change document.

2. *Create a file or files that contain the margins, headings, footers, and predefined formats used in each volume of the proposal.* Use this file as a template. Change the header or footer to indicate the new date.

3. *Create a directory labeled "Change1."* This is where you will put your first set of change pages.

4. *Place your template in the Change1 directory.* Create subdirectories for each volume of the proposal that will have change pages.

For each change page:

1. *Make a copy of your template file.*

2. *In your change document, place a hard page break at the end of the page immediately before the page you will be changing.* Place a second hard page break at the bottom of the page you will be changing.

3. *Copy the text of the old page to your template.* In your change document, highlight the old page using color or strikeout so that you will easily be able to identify which pages have been changed and which have not been changed.

4. *Save your new file in the appropriate Change1 subdirectory.* Use the page number as the file name, for example, 191.

5. *Turn on the revision feature in your software.*

6. *Make the necessary changes.*

7. *If your changes result in large blank spaces, it is traditional to include a notation that reads something like the following: This space is intentionally blank.* Another tradition in responding to paragraphs that are deleted by the government in an amendment to the RFP is to enter the word "Deleted" at the corresponding paragraph on a change page.

8. *Change the page numbers manually.* If your changes run over the first page, you will probably need to change the page numbers manually to add a hyphen and your extension, such as A, B or 1, 2 (22-A, 22-B or 22-1, 22-2).

When you print this page or these pages, make sure that the text begins and ends with the same words that the old page began and ended with—unless, of course, you made changes at the beginning or ending of the page.

Repeat this process for every change page. In the end, you will have a subdirectory that holds your full set of change pages for a particular volume. Your files will stack up sequentially. Copy your printed pages to colored paper.

## Making Changes to Change Pages

This process gets more complex when you must make changes to change pages. To do this, you check your change document to see whether or not a page has been changed. Remember, once you copy a change from the document, you mark it with a color or strike-through so that you immediately know where changes have been made.

Then you follow the soft-copy trail, checking first in the Change1 directory, next in the Change2 directory, and so forth. When you find the last version of the change page, you follow the same procedures outlined above to create a new page and a new set of change pages in a new directory.

When you create new changes on existing change pages, keep in mind that you must retain the old change bars in paragraphs that were changed before but will not be changed again, as illustrated in Example 10-5.

**Example 10-5:** Sample Successive Change Pages

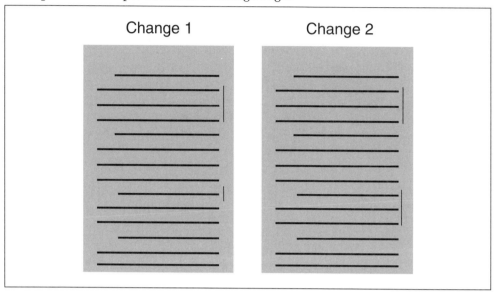

Consider this fact when you are setting your software revision feature. In my software, you can choose to "accept" revisions, in which case the software removes the change bar. You *do not* want to do that.

Once you've delivered your original or changed proposal, clean up after yourself as soon as possible, deleting any extraneous materials, such as graphics that were not used or duplicate files that were created for temporary backup. These will just create confusion—and stress—if you need to return to the document to make additional changes.

Keep one or two copies of your submissions in the proposal library—with all change pages inserted—so that you can see exactly what you submitted to the government.

# CHAPTER 11

# Planning an Oral Presentation

Increasingly, the government requires an oral presentation as part of the proposal. Oral presentations typically involve some government-dictated number of presenters from corporate and project-based staff. These presenters have a prescribed number of hours to work their way through a set of colored slides produced on PowerPoint® or similar software and run on a laptop-driven projector. Like other proposal text, the slides follow an outline provided by the government in Section L of the RFP. Slides are usually submitted with the written proposal, and the presentation itself is delivered at a later date. Slides cannot be altered between the time the written proposal is submitted and the time the presentation is made.

Though developing slides is no less or more complex than developing a written proposal, the human element involved in oral presentations calls for more planning than normal on the front end and practice on the back end. Your goal is to structure the process to minimize conflict and maximize the quality of the presentation.

## SELECTING PARTICIPANTS

The challenge of an oral presentation is that a person, prompted only by a slide or assisted by notes, must deliver a directed message to an audience of government evaluators whose sole job is to judge the quality of that message. If that scenario causes you to shiver, suffice it to say that it also sends chills down the spines of many competent and otherwise articulate project staffers. These folks—perfectly capable of handling the technical and managerial details of a government project—are far less comfortable explaining those details to a live government audience.

It is the capture manager's job to select a team of presenters that satisfies the government's head-count requirements and best delivers your company's message. It is the proposal manager's job to develop a process for crafting the message that provides for the best delivery with the least discomfort. It is also the proposal manager's job to alert inexperienced capture managers to some of the unique aspects of planning for oral presentations. Some of these are discussed below.

## Explore the Ramifications of Using Conditional Employees

Conditional employees are individuals who agree to accept a position at some time in the future if your company wins a specific contract. It is fairly easy to propose a conditional employee for a project position if that person has no obligation other than providing a résumé and signing an agreement to take the position if your company wins. It is much more difficult to propose a conditional employee if that person must be part of a presentation team. Conditional employees may not want or be able to devote the time necessary to prepare for and deliver a presentation, particularly if they are gainfully employed elsewhere.

In a worst-case scenario, you may be forced to pass over an otherwise qualified candidate because she or he is not available to prepare and present the oral part of the proposal. But you can investigate other options before you arrive at that decision. Perhaps you can persuade a conditional employee to use vacation time to prepare for the oral presentation in exchange for a reward at a later date. Make sure that you stay within any legal guidelines associated with the procurement and, of course, always produce what you promise.

## Match the Outline to the Presenter Skills

It is best to consider in advance the skills of the various candidate presenters and where those skills best fit into the government's outline. "In advance" is the operative phrase here, because some people are less than objective about the level of their skills; others don't see their skills as they fit into the whole of the presentation. Stepping lightly around egos is always tricky, but this is a place to do it, because the rewards or penalties are great.

In your planning sessions with the capture manager, assess the level of skill of each of the presenter candidates and analyze where each will fit into the government's outline. At a later date, present your findings to the candidate team, with the caveat that you will accept counter-suggestions but won't guarantee that you will use them.

## Integrate Presenters into the Proposal Process

Oral presentations often demand the involvement of individuals who are not familiar with the proposal process and sometimes don't understand how proposals are developed and evaluated. Remind the capture manager to include presenters in important steps of the proposal process, such as the kickoff meeting and brainstorming sessions, while keeping them away from information they don't need. Presenters usually have enough information to absorb without confusing them with extraneous material.

## SUPPORTING THE PRESENTATION PROCESS

In my experience, developing a presentation differs from developing a written proposal because of the sheer number of people involved and their individual personalities. On the one hand, you want to create a presentation that comes easily for each of the presenters—one that assists the presenter in delivering a smooth presentation. On the other hand, you want the presentation to hold together as a complete and whole entity that follows the government's outline and is consistent. These primary objectives tend to create a natural tension between the formal and the personal. In any group of presenters you may have one who reads the slides verbatim, another who reads her notes, and yet another who looks at the slides while seemingly talking to another point altogether. The trick, from my perspective, is to maintain the outline and a consistent format while bringing the presenters closer together in their personal styles.

An important part of this process is allowing presenters to have some say in how the information will be presented on the slide without giving the presenters total control. One way to do this is by limiting the input to two sessions, including a brainstorming session to develop the main concepts and a draft review, where comments are accepted. Between the two, an assigned writer creates the draft slides to meet the outline and formatting requirements as well as generally accepted presentation guidelines. If the government does not stipulate a format, these include the following:

- The slide background should be a light color.

- The slide font should be dark color.

- Bullet fonts should be no smaller than 18 points.

- Bullet fonts should be serif (such as Times) rather than sans serif (such as Helvetica).

As with any other part of a proposal, you will want to create styles for headings, bullets, sub-bullets, and any other standard parts of the presentation. Because the presentation will be in use as it evolves, it is important to create the format in advance so that presenters become familiar with the material and immediately recognize the slides they will present.

Creating a format for presentation graphics is problematic. In fact, it is extremely difficult to translate proposal graphics, such as large organization charts and detailed milestone charts, into graphics that are readable on a slide. You are faced with an even greater problem if the government restricts the number of slides you can use.

My advice is to do the best you can within the limits of the software and the audience. At a minimum, include in your style guide the following guidelines for presentation graphics:

- *Background color of graphics.* Use no more than two or three colors and alternate between or among them to relieve the eye but create consistency over the presentation.

- *Font to be used, including minimum size and colors.* Use the same font in all graphics.

Keep in mind that you might find yourself using graphics that you know will be unreadable, including items such as the aforementioned organization charts, phase-in charts, or project schedules. Don't worry—you are not the first person to do this, nor will you be the last. Simply make sure that the presenters understand the audience limitations and can pull out the most important elements for discussion.

In your planning sessions with the capture manager, obtain agreement about when and how the presenters will participate in the process, review the style guide that you've created, and answer the following questions:

- How many practice sessions will be needed?

- How many hours will be needed for each session?

- What room and equipment will be required for each practice session— computer, projector, projection screen? Some of the newer screens are formatted for high-definition television; they are much wider than the older screens and will distort a typical PowerPoint® presentation.

- Do you want to videotape practice sessions? If so, do you have video-tape equipment and personnel on hand? If not, do you have rental access? Can you find people who know how to videotape among the presenters?

- When will the videotapes be played back, and what equipment will be needed?

- What type of notes will be required for each presenter? What is your role—or the presenters' roles—in preparing those notes? Will notes be prepared in the software used for the presentation? If not, what software will be used?

- Do you want to hire a presentation consultant? If so, for how many sessions, and at what part of the proposal process? If you're trying to get the biggest effect for the least cost, I suggest that you hire a consultant for two sessions: the first to provide general direction in crafting your message, and the second to review your videotape or watch a practice session and provide pointers on message delivery.

- Do you want to hold a separate dress rehearsal and one or more reviews for the presentation, independent of the reviews of the written proposal? If so, who will attend, and when will they be scheduled?

- Who will be running the projector during the actual presentation? Does that person require any special training?

- Will the presentation team need any additional equipment, such as a pointer?

Once you have answered these questions, you can integrate the schedule for the presentation into that for the entire proposal. I suggest that you create an independent timeline for the presentation development and delivery, however, so that presenters who are not involved in the rest of the proposal process can see a clear line of events.

In planning for the practice sessions, think isolation. Nothing impedes practice like everyday intrusions. If possible, select a conference room that is away from everyday interference, and encourage presenters to make themselves unavailable to the workaday world.

## PRODUCING THE PRESENTATION

Production is production is production, but some types of production take longer than others. Presentation slides with memory-hogging pictures, graphics, and color content take longer to print than most proposal pages. Remember this when planning the final production schedule.

And heighten your quality control. It's one thing to discover an embarrassing error after a proposal is submitted; it's double humiliation to know that the error is going to be presented on an overhead slide by a team of your peers who will have to re-experience your embarrassment in front of government evaluators.

**Moving the Presentation to the Laptop**

There are two ways to include graphics and pictures in presentations. One is by placing a copy of the graphics item into the presentation, and another is by linking the graphics item to the presentation file. Either method can create problems if you don't load and check your software before the final presentation.

*Using linked files.* The theory behind linking a graphic item to the presentation rather than placing an actual copy in the file is to limit the size of the presentation file. A link is formed by creating a pointer in the presentation software from the presentation file to the graphics item. Theoretically, the linked graphics item can be located at any address on a computer hard drive or a connected network. When the presentation file is opened, the software checks to see if the linked graphics are available.

The problem with linking the presentation file to the graphics items is that if you move the presentation file—in this instance from a network or hard drive to the laptop—you must move all the graphics with it and re-link the graphics so that all the graphics items are available to your presentation. Otherwise, the presentation software can't locate the graphics items. Re-linking is not a difficult job if you have placed all the graphics items close to your presentation file. It is a problem if you have selected items from various locations on your hard drive or network and, at the last minute, you must move them one by one to the laptop.

The moral of this story is that you should create your presentation file in a folder called "Oral Presentation." Within that folder, create a subfolder for your presentation file and a second subfolder for your graphics. When you are ready to set up your final presentation, copy the Oral Presentation folder to the laptop, and check the links, following the instructions in your software manual. Remember that if you practice before your presentation file is finalized, you will have to repeat this process every time you copy the presentation folder to the desktop.

*Using copied files.* If you've taken the other tack and have placed copies of the graphics items into the presentation file, you will have no problem with linking because you have no links, but you should test the presentation file several times to make sure that the file doesn't overload the laptop's memory. A 128-megabyte memory should handle most presentations.

## Creating a Desktop Icon

To ease the job of the computer operator, create a direct connection to the presentation file on the laptop's desktop. With the desktop icon in place, the operator can launch the presentation software simply by double-clicking on the icon.

## Scheduling Practice for the Computer Operator

Make certain that the computer operator is someone who doesn't easily fluster, and schedule at least two practice sessions in the week before the presentation to review the procedures for setting up the computer and projector. At least one of the practice sessions should coincide with a presenter practice so that the computer operator becomes accustomed to the pace of the presentation.

The other session should allow time to play with the projector controls. I have experienced more than one occasion when the color setting on a projector was out of whack, so that the presentation file appeared with a pink or green tint. The process for clearing up this problem is one of pushing little triangular buttons on the top of the projector to access the color control—enough to drive a pressured person to distraction. On another occasion the computer refused to "talk" to the projector, for no obvious reason. I'm sure I'm not alone in experiencing these glitches.

If you must, put adhesive colored dots on the "male" and "female" parts of equipment that are intended to connect together, and run through the remedies for common problems, such as those described above. Also, arrange with the government to set up the computer and projector early on the scheduled presentation day, and pack the projector instruction manual with the projector, just in case.

## Keeping Up with Gadgetry

Ask your computer supplier about the latest in presentation gadgetry. Though I've not seen all the various types of remote controllers on the market, I'm sure there are many available, and you may want to use them. Still, unless you have a computer and projector whiz on your presentation staff, it's best to appoint a non-presenter to control the equipment, if only for setup. Then the presenters can concentrate on their presentations rather than hardware and software.

**Building Your Presentation Library**

As oral presentations become a more popular part of the proposal process, you may want to build a library of materials that can help presenters through stressful times. These can include books on structuring oral presentations, tips for relieving stress before the big performance, and hints for connecting with the audience. Many of these are easily available on the Internet.

# CHAPTER 12

# *Controlling Day-to-Day Work*

Much of what you do to de-stress your proposal life happens before or after the proposal team blows through your office. In between, you need to manage.

I find that different management styles apply to different phases in the process. A bit of micromanagement doesn't hurt and is probably necessary at the beginning and end of the process. Some breathing room is appropriate in the middle.

## BRAINSTORMING

Brainstorming jump-starts the proposal process. It is a good way to get initial ideas for storyboards, to generate ideas for incomplete sections, and to repair sections that have gone awry. It is also a good way to ensure that individuals who are having difficulty making progress get the support they need.

Use brainstorming at the beginning of the proposal process and throughout, whenever you want to focus many heads on one problem.

## USING STAND-UP MEETINGS

Stand-up meetings are brief get-togethers, usually in the morning, in which the proposal team quickly reports progress or problems. These are useful at the beginning or end of the proposal process and when approaching reviews. They can be suspended in the middle of the proposal process to allow writers some breathing space for expanding on their ideas.

To hold a stand-up meeting, schedule the meeting with all proposal team members and arrange a conference call with team members at other locations. Then follow these steps:

- *Create a master table of all proposal team members.* See Example 12-1. Make plenty of copies of the table for future use.

**Example 12-1:** Sample Stand-up Tracking Table

| Section | Author | Problem | Resolution Team/Date |
|---------|--------|---------|----------------------|
| 1.2.1 | Jim Hunter | No resource for programming | Jim, Tony, Nancy 1/27 |
| 1.2.2 | Jane Anderson | n/a | n/a |
| 1.2.3 | Larry Michaels | Benchmarking data are inconclusive | Larry, Jim 1/28 |

- *At the meeting, work your way through the list.* Hand-write a date at the top of the table. Ask each member of the proposal team if he has problems to report or resolve.

- *Provide an on-the-spot resolution to each problem or schedule a specific time and individuals to resolve the issue.* Mark these by hand in the table.

- *Use a new table for each meeting.* Review the old tables to make sure that individuals have followed up as scheduled. Cross off issues that are resolved and file old tables as all issues on that table are resolved.

You can also track issues using a spreadsheet program. To do so, create your table in a spreadsheet program, entering data into the appropriate column after the meeting. Leave space to add new items as they arise. The printout from one stand-up meeting then serves as the agenda for the next.

## GETTING MANAGEMENT SUPPORT

In the beginning of this book, I tell you how to enroll your managers and capture managers in creating a proposal process that produces winning proposals without stress. If you have taken the suggested steps, you should be able to rely on their help at the first sign of a problem with any team member. But before you ask for management help, clarify the problem and provide possible solutions.

For example, if a team member is lagging behind in producing her sections, ask directly what the problems are: Not enough time? Not enough information? Not the right information? Lack of skill in sorting through the information? No enthusiasm for the project? Solutions might involve hiring a temporary writer, assigning another in-house person to the job, holding a brainstorming session to provide direction, or setting up meetings with other experts.

If the problem person is a senior-level employee, request that the capture manager ask the questions and offer solutions, but act on the matter immediately.

## KEEPING UP

Managing the proposal process involves all the traditional management roles associated with people, costs, and schedules. Your most important role in each is keeping up—with people, costs, and schedules. If you don't know what people are doing day to day, you simply can't do your job.

The proposal coordinator doesn't have to hover over proposal team members or hold meeting after meeting to track progress. You can keep abreast in other informal ways. Without getting into lengthy discussions, ask casually how meetings have gone or if proposal team members have everything they need. Drop by the recluse at the end of the hall to touch base. Manage complaints and problems by writing them down, handling them one at a time, and checking them off the list.

## COMPILING A DRAFT

As noted in Chapter 8, compile an up-to-date copy of each volume of the proposal, with graphics, on a regular basis between reviews. Skim this work-in-progress to make sure that contributors are making the headway they report; that the theme statements, action captions, and figures are evolving; and that the writing conveys the necessary information.

## SUPERVISING PROPOSAL PERSONNEL

I've observed proposal coordinators who lead stress-free lives at the expense of everyone else on the development and production staffs, living out the "I did it, now you have to do it" proposal philosophy. I don't subscribe to that philosophy. This guide promotes the idea that all participants on the proposal process can and should lead stress-free lives while producing winning proposals.

Achieving this goal is difficult if you don't directly supervise the individuals whose services you use—particularly production personnel. Production personnel often take the brunt of proposal stress because they perform their magic at the end of the process. If someone up the line misses a deadline, this lapse can snowball until the production personnel are backed into a corner.

No one who is in a corner is likely to emerge smiling, and production personnel are no exception. Angry production personnel who are over-worked and undervalued have a way of subverting a smooth proposal process. On one of my consulting jobs, for example, a graphic artist who had grown tired of repeated late-night work told the proposal team that no more graphic changes were allowed. Unfortunately, if the subject proposal was going to have any chance of winning, the changes had to be made. She was not happy, and we were not happy to push. It was a bad situation that could and should have been avoided.

Your interest in the lives and work environment of the production staff will not only make a difference on every proposal, but it could be the deciding factor in whether or not personnel burn out over time and whether or not you need to train new personnel to meet your requirements year after year.

One of the best ways to support personnel who work with you—whether or not you supervise them directly—is to make sure that others in the process before them keep their word, that schedules don't slip, and that production personnel aren't held responsible for others' failures. Additional ways are as follows:

- *Employ flextime.* Arrange with higher-level managers to allow production personnel to follow unusual schedules as needed to complete proposals on an ongoing basis.

- *Suggest that production personnel have special compensatory time arrangements.* Many companies have comp-time policies that cause employees to lose compensatory time that is not used from paycheck to paycheck or month to month. Some companies can't formally track more than one formula for compensatory time. If this is the case with your company, arrange with your managers to employ an informal compensatory tracking system so that personnel can take the leave they deserve.

- *Always plan for backup personnel.* Sometimes the best laid plans go awry. Line up temporary personnel who can back up the production personnel if the work looks unmanageable. Pay a little bit more to get the best.

- *Give ample praise.* Production personnel are usually some emotional or physical distance away from the proposal team. Often they are not even notified if the proposal wins. Keep them in the loop by commending them for a job well done and acknowledging their work with higher-level managers.

- *Address problems.* Don't hesitate to point out work or attitude problems and to discuss them thoroughly with the individual involved. Some people are not cut out for the detail work and iterative nature of proposals. Let them know that this is a matter of poor matching between person and job, not an intrinsic flaw.

- *Fire people who don't work out.* Some people just love to make themselves miserable in any number of ways. These people can get in the way of a successful proposal process by failing to ask for what they need, complaining to others, and spreading negative attitudes. If you can't draw such people out by example, ask them to move along.

What you do for others in the proposal process returns to you many-fold.

## USING CONSULTANTS

When I first went out on my own, my goal was to develop a temporary agency for graphic artists, desktop publishers, editors, and word processors who work on the Macintosh. My idea was to focus on the high end of the market, working only with people who were the best in the business and with companies who wanted to pay for the best. I quickly found that the companies I contacted didn't want to pay for the best; they simply wanted to get someone—anyone—in a set price range.

My temporary company never got off the ground, and instead I wandered into the proposal consulting business. I base my thinking about consultants on both experiences.

### Weighing Advantages and Disadvantages

The advantages of using consultants to write and produce proposals are:

- Consultants have no competing work.

- Consultants are there when you want them and gone when you don't.

- Consultants do what they do again and again, so their skills often surpass those of in-house staff.

- Production consultants can sometimes be cheaper than in-house staff, particularly if a fully developed production shop is billing your division for its costs.

Disadvantages include the following:

- Your favorite consultant may not be available when needed.

- Good consultants are sometimes more expensive than in-house staff.

- If you can't retain a limited set of consultants on a consistent basis, you will need to train each new consultant.

- Consultants may be emotionally detached from the outcome of your proposal.

Another disadvantage of using consultants is that some live off poor proposal processes and crises. People who make a living from other people's crises have little incentive to support a workable proposal process or a stress-free environment. For this reason, I suggest coming to a "meeting of the minds."

## Coming to a Meeting of the Minds

Because consultants *are* consultants, their work tends to be erratic or sporadic. Work comes; work goes. This cyclical nature of consulting can act against the successful proposal process in that some consultants like to work long hours during the times they are working so that those hours and the associated money will carry them through dry times.

Remember that the goal of this guide is producing winning proposals without stress. Also keep in mind that overworking—on anyone's part for whatever reason—is not in the best interests of your process or your proposal. Nobody produces at his maximum working long hours day after day.

If you want to use consultants for your proposals, fill them in on your agenda of creating a winning proposal in a stress-free environment. Let them know that you plan to size the job so that no one works over eight hours a day and that you will revisit that sizing estimate as the proposal progresses, adding people if necessary. Make sure that you agree on this strategy, and keep your word.

## Getting What You Pay For

I retain my belief that you get what you pay for in consultants. Exceptions to this rule do exist, and I have worked with or after some of them—the consultant who worked an outrageous number of hours with little to show for them and the consultant who wrote a construction proposal having so many deficiencies that the company's vice president and I had to rewrite the entire document. I hope I never run into them again.

I can tell you, however, that several of the consultants I've worked with are twice as fast and twice as good as other consultants who carry price tags that are only slightly lower. Explore if you haven't found that special person yet.

On long-term projects, when reviews are few and far between, check consultants' progress regularly, matching their hours to the product. If you don't see a match, start asking questions.

## Checking References

If you're going to pay someone big money to work for you, the least you can do is check references by calling at least two corporate clients. Question the references in detail about the work performed, the hours charged, the resulting document, and deficiencies reported by the government. I consider reported deficiencies to be a better judge of a person's work than the ultimate award, simply because cost is often a highly weighted factor in many awards, and consultants have little to do with cost.

Then watch new consultants closely as they begin work. My one experience in firing a consultant involved a young woman with a great résumé. Apparently her in-house work didn't translate into the consulting environment because she was unable to move beyond the planning stage. She planned, she plotted, she talked, but she didn't produce. After several days of hemming and hawing, I asked her to leave.

## Recognizing Consultants' Strengths and Weaknesses

A few consultants can do any job under any circumstances. Most consultants do some jobs better than others and work best in certain environments. For example, I'm better at writing technical proposals than management proposals. I also work well independently and become obnoxious if I'm micromanaged.

The people who hire me again and again recognize these skills and personality traits, usually because I inform them. It took some time and a few not-so-pleasant experiences to gain understanding of myself, to understand my relationship with customers, and to convey that understanding with self-assurance. I really wanted to be able to do it all.

In one regrettable situation, I was more experienced in developing and writing proposals than the capture manager. As a fairly assertive person, I took matters into my own hands when I thought the process or the proposal was going astray. As a result, the capture manager and her managers felt that she was losing control of the proposal. And they were right. Ultimately, she and I decided that we were not a good match. I told her that I was uncomfortable with—and sometimes incapable of—following instructions that I didn't agree with. She wanted someone who would do just that: follow instructions. We parted ways.

The proposal coordinator is in a position to notice who works best under what situations. Keep your eyes open, and you will do yourself and your consultants a favor.

## Retaining Control of Your Product

Which leads me to another moral of the same story. The best way to retain control over your proposal is to be intimately familiar with it. The capture manager I mentioned above was trying to work pricing and proposal development at the same time. While juggling those responsibilities, she lost track of the proposal narrative and never got back to it. When the clarifications and deficiencies list arrived, she still hadn't read the proposal in its entirety. Don't trap yourself or other people by turning over your responsibility and power to someone else.

**Pricing Jobs According to Skills Required Rather than Level of Experience**

I price consulting jobs by the type of job rather than the experience of the consultant. Résumés and past performance sections require a lower level of skill because they are highly structured. Technical and management pieces require a higher level of skill because they are less structured. Proposal coordinators and volume managers require a still higher level of skill because these positions involve broader knowledge and supervisory capabilities.

*[handwritten annotations in right margin: $45/HR$, $55/HR$, $#65/HR$]*

This pricing structure makes sense from consulting and customer perspectives. The customer pays one rate for a consultant who is preparing résumés, another rate for the same consultant working on the technical volume, and a third rate if the same consultant is serving as a proposal coordinator or volume manager. The customer doesn't pay for expertise that is not used.

## LOGGING AMENDMENTS

*Amendments* are changes to the RFP issued after the RFP is released and sometimes issued *after* the proposals have been submitted. *Clarification requests* and *deficiency reports*, addressed below, are individualized sets of questions that the government sometimes sends to each offeror.

The proposal coordinator is responsible for maintaining a current version of the RFP and is therefore responsible for logging amendments so that the full RFP is always available for reference. If the government provides change pages, pull out old pages from the RFP and replace them with new pages. File the old pages for safekeeping, just in case you must refer to them later.

If the government provides paragraph-by-paragraph changes, cross out the old paragraph and insert the new one by physically stapling the new on the old so that you can still compare the two if you have to. Or slip a page containing the new paragraph behind the page containing the old one.

This is one place where a soft copy of the RFP can be valuable in that you can create a new, clean document by making a copy of the original RFP, deleting old paragraphs, and typing in the new or pasting new copy from a scanned file.

I am not yet prepared, however, to rely on a soft-copy version of the RFP. If you do as advised in the last paragraph, keep a set of hard-copy updates as well.

### Responding to Clarifications and Deficiencies

Clarification requests and deficiency reports are a normal part of the process in large hardware bids. They are more rare in smaller bids for services and systems. Clarification requests are an attempt to gather more or better information about the offeror's bid. Deficiency reports are the government's indication that reviewers don't think the product or service offered meets the government requirements. Sometimes CRs and DRs are fishing for specific words or phrases from the RFP rather than supplementary information.

CRs and DRs can also be cryptic. Sometimes the government only hints at what they want in the questions they ask. In this case, only a person who is intimately familiar with the customer or ferrets out the subtle underlying meaning can choose words for an appropriate response. If they are so cryptic that no one understands what the government is fishing for, you should ask the government to restate the question. You may or may not get a clearer restatement.

Usually the proposal team is reconstituted to respond to CRs and DRs, with good reason: This may be the last opportunity to explain a product or to repair damage done. Responding to CRs and DRs should not be a situation where you "wing it"; your response must be just right.

### Reviewing Responses to Clarification Requests and Deficiency Reports

Responses to CRs and DRs could make or break your proposal and should be subject to review, as described in Chapter 9. At a minimum, reviewers should include the capture manager, technical lead, and an individual who can commit on behalf of the company.

When you hold a CR and DR review, provide each reviewer with a set of responses and associated change pages along with a full proposal so that reviewers can place change pages in context.

## SUBMITTING THE BEST AND FINAL OFFER

The best and final offer, or BAFO, can be submitted with or without change pages. It can be submitted informally, as an attachment to a letter that acknowledges the government's request for BAFO, or formally, as change pages to the price proposal.

Follow the government's instructions. Most pricing specialists take BAFO into consideration when they prepare their original numbers for the price proposal. They pad the numbers in a few of the pricing categories, but not so many as to price the company out of the competitive range—with the intention of unpadding them when BAFO is submitted.

## CLEANING UP

Once every question is answered and the very, very best and final offer has been submitted, the proposal manager moves on to the next project while tracking the proposals that have been submitted and are awaiting award. Some agencies call the contract awardee, following up with letters to the winner and losers; other agencies notify all parties by mail. Whichever way you receive notice, the contract award isn't the end of the process. You'll want to notify all concerned, from the capture manager to the desktop publisher, of the results of their work. Congratulations on good work are in order either way.

If you won, you may want to plan a celebration for all involved, to reinforce their membership in the winning team and boost their spirits for the next effort.

If you've lost, you'll want to schedule a debriefing with the agency involved. A formal debriefing is provided to any bidding company that requests one under the FAR. The debrief meeting is an opportunity for losing parties to ask the evaluators exactly how their proposals fared with respect to the stated evaluation factors in Section M of the RFP. If that agency is some distance away, the debriefing can take the form of a conference call arranged in advance.

The proposal debriefing will be most productive if you write out questions in advance, reminding yourself of the evaluation factors and questioning the evaluators on any issues that you don't understand. For example:

*Section M allocates 25 points to the Technical Proposal. How many points did Company A receive? In what areas and for what reasons were points deducted?*

Focus on how your proposal stacked up in each of the areas of evaluation and where the document fell short. Ask the government to be precise about where the proposal was lacking, and listen carefully to what the evaluators say.

Then don't take the comments too seriously unless the evaluation goes to the heart of proposal compliance. Selection authorities vary to extremes across industries and agencies. If the selection authority found the proposal noncompliant in any way, however, examine the issue very closely. If your price was close to that of the winning proposal or less than that of the winning proposal, you may have an issue that is worth protesting.

Alternatively, you may have an issue with your proposal process if you find in retrospect that your proposal was indeed noncompliant.

## Lodging a Protest

Proposal protests are legal proceedings that are handled by law firms specializing in government procurements and contracts. You can guess then that protests can be costly undertakings that are not lodged on a whim. If you think you have a valid reason for protest, ask your corporate lawyer to contact a law firm that specializes in such protests—I imagine there are more in Washington, D.C., than in other regions of the country—and follow their instructions. If a protest is indeed valid, the lawyers will take charge, and thereafter the proposal coordinator and capture manager will probably be called upon to answer questions.

## Moving and Deleting Files

Once your proposal is submitted, you'll want to delete all the files that are not final versions of documents. Clean out old versions, unused graphics, and administrative materials that don't need to be archived.

## Reviewing Boilerplate

Update your boilerplate. If you have written the best operations plan ever or created a new graphic that can be used repeatedly, make sure you place it in your boilerplate folder.

Then relax, pat your staff on the back, and take some time off.

# *Afterword*

As I was wrapping up this book, I was also wrapping up a 300-and-some page proposal. The proposal represented a must-win bid for our small division, so the entire administrative staff was involved in some way.

The vice president, in his inimitable fashion, just *had* to make last-minute revisions to the past performance section because it was the lead-in to the proposal; an operations manager, who led definition of the technical solution, was scheduled for not-to-be-changed vacation two days before the proposal was due, and he was writing until the moment he left; a consultant bottomed out on us—my irritability was involved—the day before delivery; and the night before the proposal was due, I was in that unfamiliar position of deciding whether it would be more productive to stay up for the night or get several hours' sleep. I chose the latter; if I had had company, however, I might have chosen the former.

"What happened here?" you might ask. In the words of the old Indian chief in "Little Big Man": "Sometimes the magic works, and sometimes it doesn't." I find solace in the fact that even an old sage cannot make things go his way every time he chooses. Some proposals will be better than others, and sometimes the process will work better than other times. Occasionally I simply tire of being a nag and let events turn as they will. Then I pick the pieces up and move on.

And I keep forcing change. Though I shudder at overused terms like "best practices" and "continuous process improvement," trying to scrub them from proposals as best I can, I do embrace their essence—the notion that little by little over time and with repeated attention, I can make big improvements to the proposal process and the lives of everyone who participates in the proposals I manage. The more organized I am, the more rested I am, the heartier I can laugh when things fall apart before my very eyes. You can do the same, and eventually your process will work like a well-oiled machine. Except when it doesn't. Then you can make adjustments and forge ahead.

Our must-win proposal was, of course, delivered on time because it had to be. While I was still showering at home on the morning of the delivery date, an assistant vice president was shopping at an office supply store for larger binders. While I was finishing up the table of contents, the team meticulously wrapped the delivery boxes so they looked better than my Christmas presents. Meanwhile, the graphic artist used the proposal cover design to create stand-out labels for the boxes. Late nights, panic, and all, this was a team effort.

I tell you, that proposal is a winner.

# APPENDIX A
# *Checklists*

## CHECKLIST A: PLANNING AND HOLDING A PRE-PROPOSAL MEETING

\_\_\_\_\_ Schedule a meeting with the capture manager and production manager that allows plenty of time to discuss the proposal thoroughly.

\_\_\_\_\_ Prepare materials to demonstrate to the capture manager and production manager how the proposal process works and what your respective jobs will be.

\_\_\_\_\_ Compile your standardized forms and instruction material for the capture manager to demonstrate how the process works.

\_\_\_\_\_ Prepare materials to explain your philosophy: winning proposal *and* stress-free environment.

\_\_\_\_\_ Provide a draft schedule for the proposal.

\_\_\_\_\_ Make a list of questions to ask the capture manager.

    \_\_\_\_\_ Who will your technical resources be, where are they located now, and where will they be located for the proposal effort?

    \_\_\_\_\_ What is the predicted turnaround time?

    \_\_\_\_\_ Is there a possibility of rewriting boilerplate, résumés, or past performance data before the RFP is released?

    \_\_\_\_\_ What support does the capture manager want in terms of writers, editors, word-processors, and technical illustrators?

    \_\_\_\_\_ Who are your corporate teammates, and who are the individuals who will serve as their point persons?

\_\_\_\_\_ Ask the production manager about availability of staff or the need for temporary employees.

### Following-up After the Pre-proposal Meeting

\_\_\_\_\_ Contact temporary personnel regarding their availability.

\_\_\_\_\_ Provide your purchasing department with the information they need for purchase orders to hire temporary employees.

\_\_\_\_\_ Create a confidentiality agreement for team personnel and consultants.

\_\_\_\_\_ Make preliminary arrangements for office space.

\_\_\_\_\_ Make preliminary arrangements for computers, network access, phones, and phone message access.

## CHECKLIST B: OUTLINING THE PROPOSAL

### Preparing to Outline the RFP

_____ Scan Sections C, L, and M and other pertinent specifications into the computer.

_____ Read Sections C, L, and M.

_____ Weigh the advantages and disadvantages of fitting Sections L and M into Section C or fitting Section C into Sections L and M.

_____ Consider what information you want to provide beside that required by the RFP. An executive summary? Section summaries?

_____ Read other sections of the RFP to see if they contain pertinent requirements.

_____ Note requirements that will affect production.

### Creating Headings and Numbers

_____ Create section (or subsection) headings that reflect headings in the RFP.

_____ Include in your outline unnumbered subsection requirements.

_____ Number your outline to track with Section C, if appropriate.

### Addressing Issues

_____ Address all outlining questions and issues with the capture manager.

### Creating a Compliance Matrix

_____ Use your outline to create a compliance matrix and assignment matrix.

## CHECKLIST C: CREATING SUPPORT MATERIAL

### Creating Support Material

_____ Investigate to see if your company has standard support materials, such as style and format guides.

_____ Create a style guide that includes the following:

    _____ Names to identify the offeror, such as the Anderson Team

    _____ Use of initial capitalization

    _____ Use of active and passive voice

    _____ Commonly misused words and corrections

    _____ Hyphenation of common computer terms

    _____ Rules for using words or numerals to express numbers

    _____ Computer application names and their formats, if your proposal is software-intensive

    _____ Appropriate acronyms, if your proposal is acronym-intensive.

_____ Create formats that include definitions of the following:

    _____ Fonts

    _____ Font styles (bold, italic, underline)

    _____ Font size

    _____ Line spacing

    _____ Paragraph spacing

    _____ Columns

    _____ Justification

    _____ Indentations.

_____ Create a format guide that provides predefined formats for the following:

    _____ Place holders for figures and tables, if they will be created in another program

    _____ Items that will be included in the table of contents and lists of figures or tables

    _____ Section headings to the four-digit level or lower

    _____ Theme statements

_____ Figure/table titles and action captions

_____ Requirements, if they will appear in the proposal narrative

_____ The proposal narrative

_____ Bullets

_____ Unnumbered subsections

_____ Headers and footers.

_____ Collect soft-copy files of previous proposals and placed them on the network or diskettes.

_____ Create a storyboard format.

_____ Create review forms.

_____ Create a graphic submittal form.

## CHECKLIST D: CREATING A CONFIGURATION CONTROL SYSTEM

### Planning a Configuration Control System

_____ Talk with your network administrator and computer support personnel so that you understand how your networked systems and applications work.

_____ Understand what capabilities are available to you for:

_____ Defining system "views" so that proposal writers have access only to those directories that you choose

_____ Defining passwords so that the logon procedures can be set up before the proposal team arrives

_____ Locking and unlocking files so that you can keep track of files that are "out" to writers.

### Configuration Control for Networked Systems

_____ Define directories for the following or your own equivalents on your networked or stand-alone system:

_____ The cost volume

_____ Administration items, such as schedules, the compliance matrix, stand-up meeting minutes, forms, agendas, etc.

_____ Background material, such as soft-copy files of technical and management methodologies, corporate hierarchies, past performance data

_____ Active files for each volume of the proposal, except cost

_____ In/Out files that will be handed to and from writers

_____ Old versions of the proposal from various phases, including storyboard and review copies.

_____ Create instructions for using the configuration control system through the Inbox and Outbox, including the following:

_____ Instructions for requesting a file

_____ Instructions for returning a file

_____ Warnings against renaming a file.

### Configuration Control for Stand-alone Systems

_____ Create a diskette for each major section or subsection of the proposal, using your preliminary list of writing assignments as a guide.

_____ Create a physical Inbox/Outbox system for managing diskettes.

### Backing Up the Proposal

_____ Talk with your network administrator to find out how often your network servers are backed up.

_____ Develop a method to back up your files daily.

## CHECKLIST E: SUPPORTING THE PROPOSAL TEAM

**Planning Support**

_____ Locate and reserve space for desks, computers, and telephones.

_____ Locate and reserve space for team meetings.

_____ Set up computer passwords and e-mail accounts.

_____ Compile the following items:

    _____ Past performance data

    _____ Corporate data on teammates

    _____ Boilerplate for management sections and methodologies

    _____ Graphics submittal form and sample graphics

    _____ A style guide

    _____ A format guide

    _____ Instructions for exchanging files.

**Setting Up Support**

_____ Organize space so that writers will not be disturbed.

_____ Provided plenty of space to spread and organize materials.

_____ Organize equipment so that each writer has phone.

_____ Set up message access for each writer.

_____ Provide a computer for each writer.

_____ Provide computer and network access codes for each writer.

_____ Distribute confidentiality agreements.

_____ Collect the confidentiality agreements.

_____ Arrange for building and office access.

_____ Call other divisions that must supply information for the proposal.

_____ Organize your networked or stand-alone directories.

_____ Create files with the following components:

     _____ Predefined text formats

     _____ Page formats

     _____ Headings and subheadings

     _____ Requirements

## CHECKLIST F: PLANNING AND HOLDING THE KICKOFF MEETING

### Scheduling the Kick-off Meeting

_____ Schedule the meeting with all proposal in-house and teammate proposal team members.

_____ Ask a senior-level manager to request the presence of all team members.

_____ Enlist the help of a senior-level manager to open the meeting and handle portions of the agenda.

_____ Schedule a conference room, overhead projector, and projection screen.

_____ Plan for refreshments.

### Planning and Holding the Kickoff Meeting

_____ Prepare slides to do the following:

     _____ Introduce teammates and the proposal team

     _____ Preview the agency and the procurement

     _____ Highlight the proposed solution

     _____ Review major discriminators

     _____ Review the proposal process

     _____ Review the proposed writing assignments

     _____ Review the proposed schedule.

_____ Develop a written agenda.

_____ Provide copies of slides to the senior-level manager and capture manager who will be participating in the meeting.

_____ Compile the following materials for the kickoff handout:

     _____ A copy of the slides that will be presented at the meeting

     _____ Past performance data

     _____ Corporate data on teammates

     _____ Boilerplate for management sections and methodologies

     _____ Graphics submittal form and sample graphics

_____ A style guide

_____ A format guide

_____ Instructions for exchanging files.

_____ Practice your presentation.

_____ Set up chairs, projector, slides, and screen.

_____ Set up refreshments.

## CHECKLIST G: DEVELOPING STORYBOARDS

### Preparing for Classic Storyboards

_____ Create a storyboard format on paper and soft copy with all the items in Checklist C.

_____ Determine if the proposal team will be working on-site throughout the proposal process.

_____ Assess the writers' levels of competence in word-processing application.

_____ Or arrange for word-processing support.

### Planning Storyboarding Sessions

_____ Schedule regular storyboarding sessions throughout the proposal process, with emphasis on the beginning of the process.

_____ Book a conference room with adequate space to move around.

_____ Equip your storyboarding room with a whiteboard or overhead projector and accessories.

_____ Arrange for modest refreshments, such as sodas and granola bars.

_____ Identify a session facilitator.

_____ Schedule "wall reviews" of storyboards throughout the proposal process.

### Holding Storyboarding Sessions

_____ Introduce members of the proposal team.

_____ Provide team members with soft-copy and hard-copy storyboard formats.

_____ Describe components of the proposal:

    _____ Theme statements

    _____ Figures and tables

    _____ Figure and table callouts

    _____ Figure and table titles

    _____ Action captions

    _____ Bullets.

_____ Explain the storyboarding and brainstorming processes.

_____ Explain features and benefits.

_____ Allow for frequent restroom and "move around" breaks.

_____ Resolve all issues that arise or plan for their resolution at another
time by identifying a responsible individual and a resolution date.

## CHECKLIST H: PLANNING AND HOLDING PROPOSAL REVIEWS

### Planning the Proposal Review

_____ Allow adequate time for thorough reviews.

_____ Select the appropriate reviewers with knowledge of all of the technical and managerial aspects of the proposal, such as:

> _____ A representative who can commit on behalf of the company

> _____ A representative from each major programmatic aspect of the solution being proposed, for example, networking, software development, and computer support; or medical and administrative

> _____ A representative of the management team for the proposed contract

> _____ A compliance reviewer.

_____ Send each reviewer a notice of the date, time, and length of the review based on your projections.

_____ Suggest that reviewers wear casual, comfortable clothes.

_____ Provide detailed instructions to reviewers.

_____ Point out what is helpful and what is damaging in review comments.

_____ Name a review facilitator to ensure that reviewers carry through with their missions.

_____ Schedule a separate résumé review if résumés are a substantial part of your bid.

### Planning a Wall Review of Storyboards

_____ Set up a schedule for the facilitator that will allow the team to review all the sections within the allotted time, with regular breaks.

_____ Appoint a timer to assist in keeping the facilitator and team on schedule.

_____ Set up tables so that all reviewers and teammates can see the storyboards—although they will not be able to read them.

_____ Contract with a caterer to provide lunch in the conference room with beverages, plates, napkins, and utensils.

_____ Stock the room with additional coffee and sodas for all tastes, and perhaps light snacks.

_____ Equip the room with a blackboard, whiteboard, or slide projector and necessary accessories, such as chalk, markers, erasers, and transparencies.

_____ Copy extra sets of the RFP and the storyboards for the forgetful.

_____ Appoint a compliance reviewer.

_____ Compile, copy, and assemble the review document as listed below.

## Planning a Wall Review of Storyboards

_____ Introduce the reviewers and teammates.

_____ Review the schedule for the day, giving goals.

_____ Remind reviewers of the instructions provided to them, including how to be constructive rather than destructive in making their remarks and suggestions.

_____ Ask the facilitator to take over the meeting, the timer to begin timing, and the first section contributor to begin taking notes.

_____ The facilitator works through all sections.

_____ The facilitator resolves all issues on the spot or identifies a responsible individual and a date for resolution.

_____ Collect any storyboard mark-ups that were not conveyed to the authors.

## Planning a Pink Team or Red Team Review

_____ If the proposal is large, break it into logical pieces and make assignments based on subject matter expertise.

_____ Estimate the time needed to review each section.

_____ Set up a schedule that will allow the team to review all the sections within the allotted time, with regular breaks.

_____ Reserve the largest room available. Consider renting a room in a nearby hotel if your own facilities are inadequate.

_____ Arrange seating for individual reading and for presentations, avoiding the single, oval conference table if you can.

_____ If the room is large enough, set up tables facing a whiteboard or projection screen *and* individual seating.

_____ Arrange reviewer seating so that they are not directly across from one another while reading.

_____ Contract with a caterer to provide lunch in the conference room with beverages, plates, napkins, and utensils.

_____ Stock the room with additional coffee and sodas for all tastes, and perhaps light snacks.

_____ Equip the room with a blackboard, whiteboard, or slide projector and necessary accessories, such as chalk, markers, and erasers, and transparencies.

**Compiling the Review Document**

_____ Compile a printout of the following materials, as appropriate:

  _____ The compliance matrix

  _____ All text sections

  _____ All graphics

  _____ The executive summary, if it is available

  _____ An inside cover page with the requisite non-disclosure statement

  _____ A draft table of contents without page numbers

  _____ A draft list of figures and tables without page numbers

  _____ Appendices

  _____ Résumés

  _____ Acronym list

  _____ Cover pages for appendices, résumés, the acronym list, etc.

_____ Assemble the front matter and text sections as they will appear in the final document.

_____ Assemble the graphics printouts sequentially by tracking number.

_____ Reduce fold-out graphics to 8.5 x 11 on the copier if they remain legible after reduction.

_____ Insert the graphics by matching the tracking number in the text file with the tracking number of the graphic printout and place the graphic printout behind the page where the figure or table will finally appear.

_____ Copy the entire set onto three-hole-punch paper.

_____ Make a set for each member of the proposal team and each member of the review team, with a few extras for emergencies.

_____ Or, if you are dividing volumes among reviewers, copy only the appropriate volume for each reviewer.

_____ Insert colored slip sheets or tabs between sections if you see an advantage in doing so.

_____ Place each review copy in a three-ring binder, with the compliance matrix on top.

_____ Slip the acronym list into the inside front pouch of the binder.

_____ Insert a draft copy of the proposal cover into the see-through cover pouch on the review binders.

### Holding the Pink Team or Red Team Review

_____ Introduce the reviewers.

_____ Review the schedule for the day.

_____ Provide reviewers with instructions and associated forms.

_____ Explain the rating scheme and how it is applied.

_____ Ask reviewers to refrain from over-copyediting.

_____ Ask for questions and comments.

_____ Make sure that all reviewers have the required documents.

_____ The facilitator answers questions, checks progress, assists the section assignees in completing the review process.

### Consolidating the Review Comments

_____ The facilitator/section representative asks each reviewer for his rating of the section.

_____ The facilitator/section representative asks each reviewer for his top three suggestions for improvements to each section.

_____ The facilitator/section representative asks each reviewer for other suggestions.

_____ The facilitator/section representative asks each reviewer for resource needs to complete the section.

_____ The facilitator/section representative writes all the responses on the whiteboard (or other equipment).

_____ The facilitator/section representative resolves discrepancies one by one.

_____ All reviewers hear/see all section reviews.

_____ The facilitator prepares slides showing the section rating, three major points for each section, other suggestions, and needed resources.

_____ The facilitator selects a presenter for each slide.

## Holding a Red Team Debriefing

_____ Introduce the reviewers and the proposal team.

_____ Pass around a sign-in sheet with the names, phone numbers, and e-mail addresses of all reviewers and proposal team members.

_____ Copy the sign-in sheet to distribute to all team members.

_____ Distribute the sign-in sheet to the reviewers.

_____ Explain that you will be walking through the slides using a section reviewer as presenter.

_____ Ask the proposal team to hold comments and questions until the presenter has completed his commentary on the slide.

_____ The facilitator mediates significant issues on the spot or identifies individuals who will resolve the issues and a resolution date.

_____ The facilitator designates an individual who will be responsible for securing resources identified by the reviewers.

_____ The facilitator reads back all the comments made during the review.

_____ Ask reviewers and the proposal team to call or e-mail the appropriate person if they have delayed reactions or suddenly come up with just the right fix for a problem section.

_____ Gather mark-ups and rating sheets from the reviewers.

_____ Thank the reviewers.

_____ Schedule a meeting to plan your recovery.

## Distributing the Review Comments

_____ Split the marked-up proposals and the rating sheets by section.

_____ Make one copy of the slides, markups, and rating sheets for safe keeping.

_____ Distribute sets of the slides, markups, and rating sheets to the section authors.

## CHECKLIST I: PRODUCING THE PROPOSAL

### Thinking About Production

\_\_\_\_\_ Inspect Section L for requirements that will have ramifications during production. Know the following:

     \_\_\_\_\_ How the proposal must be paginated (within each section vs. straight through the document)

     \_\_\_\_\_ How many pages the proposal will have

     \_\_\_\_\_ How large figures are to be presented

     \_\_\_\_\_ If the proposal is to be submitted in soft-copy format, and if so, in what format (Word for Windows, WordPerfect)

     \_\_\_\_\_ If your company must provide any other soft-copy items, such as sample products or demonstration programs

     \_\_\_\_\_ If your proposal must include glossy brochures, user manuals, specification sheets, or similar material on the products you are proposing. If so, how many?

     \_\_\_\_\_ If you must prepare elements of your proposal for a stand-up presentation rather a printed document

     \_\_\_\_\_ If you must provide a sanitized copy of the cost proposal.

\_\_\_\_\_ Know what your proposal will look like by choice. Answer these questions:

     \_\_\_\_\_ Are you using any or many 11 x 17-inch or similar foldouts?

     \_\_\_\_\_ If so, how will you be placing the titles and page numbers on these foldouts?

     \_\_\_\_\_ Will you be typing them in a separate file and physically pasting them up?

     \_\_\_\_\_ Will the graphic artist be typing the title into the graphics file?

     \_\_\_\_\_ Do you have an in-house capability to reproduce 11 x 17-inch pages?

     \_\_\_\_\_ Will you be folding these large pages by hand or instead handing this terribly boring process over to a professional print shop?

     \_\_\_\_\_ Are you including by choice any unwieldy documents as appendices or support material? How will you present them?

_____ Are you including any other items that require special production, handling, or packaging?

_____ How will you be packing the proposal? Do you need to order boxes, tape, and labels?

## Scheduling Production

_____ Investigate your in-house capabilities for producing covers, spines, and tabs.

_____ Order binders.

_____ Order covers and spines to fit the binders.

_____ Order tabs.

_____ Order paper.

_____ Order packing materials.

_____ Schedule times to check binders.

_____ Schedule times to check covers and spines.

_____ Schedule times to check tabs.

_____ Schedule times to check paper.

_____ Allow for production time before the storyboard review.

_____ Allow for production time before the Pink Team review.

_____ Allow for production time before the Red Team review.

_____ Allow for production time before delivery.

_____ Schedule editors.

_____ Schedule graphic support.

_____ Schedule word processors.

_____ Contact a vendor or schedule in-house reproduction.

## Producing the Proposal for Reviews

_____ Assemble the front matter and text sections as they will appear in the final document.

_____ Assemble the graphics printouts sequentially by tracking number.

_____ Reduced fold-out graphics to 8.5 x 11 on the copier if they remain legible after reduction.

_____ Insert graphics by matching the tracking number in the text file with the tracking number of the graphic printout.

_____ Place the graphic printout behind the page where the figure or table will finally appear.

_____ Copy the entire set on three-hole-punch paper.

_____ Make a set for each member of the proposal team and each member of the review team, with a few extras for emergencies.

_____ Or, if you are dividing volumes among reviewers, copy the appropriate volume/section for each reviewer.

_____ Insert colored slip sheets or tabs between sections if you see an advantage in doing so.

_____ Place each review copy in a three-ring binder, with the compliance matrix on top.

_____ Insert a draft copy of the proposal cover into the see-through cover pouch on the review binders.

**Flowing the Text and Placing the Graphics**

_____ Place all text.

_____ Place all graphics after the callout.

_____ Check all figure and table titles and action captions.

_____ Check the top and bottom of each page for widow and orphan lines.

_____ Split tables that run over pages, creating (1 of 2) and (2 of 2) tables.

_____ Compile odd-ball graphics.

_____ Complete the following front matter and appendices for each volume:

    _____ The signed transmittal letter

    _____ Inside cover pages with disclosure statements

    _____ Tables of contents

    _____ Lists of figures and tables

    _____ Acronym lists

_____ Any appendices, including résumés and support material

_____ Cover pages for all of the above.

_____ Compile appendices

_____ Assemble the inside body of the proposal

_____ Make all copies required by the RFP and extras for your proposal team.

_____ Make a sanitized version of the cost proposal, if required.

_____ Assemble the binders, covers, and spines for each volume.

_____ Number each copy of each volume with a copy number, if required.

_____ Insert the body of the proposal and the tabs.

_____ Check each page of each proposal.

_____ Package and label the proposal in quantities required by the RFP.

# APPENDIX B

# *Samples*

## SAMPLE A: MODIFIED STORYBOARD FORMAT

### Section 1: Management

### 1.1 Managing Task Order Contracts

**Requirement: L.3.1 Explain your company's organization and management procedures for managing task order contracts. (M.3.1 restates this requirement.)**

> *Theme Statement: Enter a theme statement here.*

> Attach a graphic here.

Enter a Figure Title:

Enter an Action Caption:

Enter Major Points Here. Link features to benefits.

- 
- 
- 
- 
-

### 1.1.1 Organizing for Task Order Contracts

*Theme Statement: Enter a theme statement here.*

Attach a graphic here.

Enter a Figure Title:

Enter an Action Caption:

Enter Major Points Here. Link features to benefits.

-
-
-
-
-

### 1.1.2 Managing with Standard Procedures for Task Order Contracts

*Theme Statement: Enter a theme statement here.*

Attach a graphic here.

Enter a Figure Title:

Enter an Action Caption:

Enter Major Points Here. Link features to benefits.

-
-
-
-

## SAMPLE B: STYLE GUIDE

### *Naming Conventions*

| | |
|---|---|
| To name our team, use: | Shannon Associates<br>the Shannon Associates team<br>We |
| To name the proposed bid, use: | the HGA program |
| To name the customer, use: | the Healthcare Agency or<br>the Agency |
| To describe our staff, use: | engineers<br>professionals |

### *Active/Passive Voice*

| | |
|---|---|
| Use active voice | We settled fifteen claims in the first week. |
| Rather than passive voice | Fifteen claims were settled in the first week. |

### *Stylistic Conventions*

| | |
|---|---|
| Use these forms of the following words: | benchmark<br>bidirectional<br>built-in (adjective)<br>burn-in (noun); burn in (verb)<br>change-out (noun); change out (verb)<br>checklist<br>checkpoint<br>coprocessor<br>courseware<br>database<br>draft-quality<br>e-mail<br>file server<br>filename<br>high-level (unit modifier)<br>high-speed (unit modifier)<br>in-house (unit modifier)<br>long-term (unit modifier)<br>menu-driven (unit modifier)<br>multiprocessing<br>multiuser |

off-line (unit modifier)
off-load (verb)
off-the-shelf (unit modifier)
real-time (unit modifier)
runtime
shutdown
standalone
testbed
timeframe
workforce
workgroup

Use these forms of the following words:

| | |
|---|---|
| online | before a noun, as in "online service" |
| | following a verb, as in "This service is on line" |
| on-site | before a noun, as in our on-site team |
| on site | after a verb, as in "Our team is on site daily" |
| logon | as an adjective or noun, as in "the logon procedure used is. . ." or "the logon consists of two steps" |
| log onto/logs onto | as a verb, as in "users log onto the system using a password" |
| back up (verb) | Back up the system at 9:00 am. |
| back-up | as a unit modifier, as in "the back-up program ran smoothly" |
| backup (noun) | We run a system backup nightly. |
| Hard-copy | as a unit modifier, as in "keep a hard-copy file" |
| hard copy | as an adjective (hard) and noun (copy) as in "print a hard copy." |
| Soft-copy | as a unit modifier, as in "it must be delivered in soft-copy format" |
| soft copy | as an adjective (soft) and noun (copy) as in "all of our files are soft copies." |

### General Rules

| | |
|---|---|
| Use active voice | We surveyed four products |
| Avoid passive voice | Four products were surveyed |
| Avoid "should" and "shall" | Use "will" |

### Word Savers

| *Use* | *Do Not Use* |
|---|---|
| many | a large portion of |
| most | a major portion of |
| concluded | arrived at the conclusion |
| always | at all times |
| soon | at an early date |
| while | during the time that |
| for May | for the month of May |
| about/concerning/regarding | in regard to |
| for | in the amount of |
| if | in the event that |
| most | maximum quantity |
| least | minimum quantity |
| engineers think | the consensus among engineers is that |
| finish | finalize |
| start | initiate |
| end | terminate |
| after | subsequent to |
| before | prior to |
| because | for the reason that |
| use | utilize |
| can | is capable of/has the capability to |
| to | in order to |
| largely | to a large extent |
| compliant | fully compliant |

### Format Issues

| | |
|---|---|
| Number figures consecutively within sections | Figure 1.1.1-1, Figure 1.1.1-2, etc. |
| Place figure titles and action captions below the figure | |
| Number tables consecutively within sections | Table 1.3-1, Table 1.3-2, etc. |
| Place table titles and action captions above the table | |
| Call out all figures and tables in the text. | Figure 9.2-1 illustrates our plan. Table 5.2.2 is a comparison of performance statistics. |
| Place figure and table placeholders after the callouts. | |
| Site sections of the RFP and proposal using this format: | RFP Section L.1.2.5 RFP Section C.3.5.9 Section 4 of this proposal |
| Leave a space between numbers and abbreviations | 20 MB |
| Use this form to introduce an acronym: | Our third customer is the National Security Agency (NSA). The NSA uses. . . |
| To make an acronym plural, use an "s" without an apostrophe | Our solution links five CPUs. |

### Initial Caps

| | |
|---|---|
| Buttons/switch/indicator names | On/Off switch Form Feed button Paper Out indicator |
| Field names | First Name field |
| Function names | the Mail Merge function |
| Specific menu names | the Format menu |
| Option names choose Paste | select Cut |
| Software components/module names | the Accounts Payable module |

| | |
|---|---|
| Formal names of facilities, systems, reviews, or government units | Mission Control Center<br>Configuration Control Board<br>Office of the Clerk |
| Program names | Space Shuttle Program |
| Table and figure titles | Figure 2-1; Table 5.3-1 |
| Section names | Section 4, Section 10 |

### Lower Case

| | |
|---|---|
| Generic references to menu names | the e-mail menu; the setup menu |
| Generic software modules | accounts receivable modules |
| Generic job titles technicians | programmers, analysts, service |

### Numbers

| | |
|---|---|
| Spell out numbers zero through nine | two computers, five programmers, nine modem ports |
| Use digits for numbers over nine, unless the number starts a sentence | We employ 50 engineers.<br>Fifty people attended the conference. |
| Use digits for units of time or measurement, including age, time, dates, decimals, degrees, percentage of proportion | 5 hours, 36 years, 15 degrees north, 50 percent |
| Use digits in unit modifiers | 5-percent increase, 32-bit processor, 2-year period |

| Singular | Plural |
|---|---|
| datum | data |
| index | indices |
| criterion | criteria |
| appendix | appendices |

## *Word Usage*

### affect, effect

affect (verb)
Example:

to influence
This delay will not ultimately affect our delivery.

effect (verb)
Example:

to bring about
We cannot effect change without some discomfort.

effect (noun)
Example:

a result
The effect of the program was dramatic.

### amount, number

amount

Example:

use for inanimate objects and things that can't be counted
The amount of gas released was unknown.

number

Example:

use for animates and things that can be counted
We will identify the number of terminals needed at a later date.

### around

This is a colloquial term for approximately or about.
Don't use it for those meanings.

### between, among

between
Example:

use to discuss two entities
The user chooses between two models of computers.

among

Example:

use to discuss more than two entities
We resolve differences through discussion among all three parties.

### Complement, compliment

complement
Example:

to supplement, to complete
Her technology background complements her training degree.

| | |
|---|---|
| compliment | to praise or flatter |
| Example: | General Brown complimented the NGO team on a thorough presentation. |

**currently, presently**

| | |
|---|---|
| currently | now |
| presently | shortly, soon |
| Example: | She is currently (not presently) the Program Manager for the NGO contract. |

**disinterested, uninterested**

| | |
|---|---|
| disinterested | impartial, showing no bias |
| uninterested | taking no interest, indifferent |
| Example: | Members of the review board should be disinterested evaluators. |

**ensure, insure, assure**

| | |
|---|---|
| ensure | guarantee |
| insure | refers to insurance; do not use to mean "guarantee." |
| assure | refers to psychological reassurance |

**fewer, less**

| | |
|---|---|
| fewer | use for items that can be counted |
| Example: | Fewer than 100 person attended the training. |
| less | use for bulk or quantity |
| Example: | The new method is far less time-consuming than the old method. |
| impact | do not use as a verb; use "affect" instead. |
| input | do not use as a verb; use "enter" instead. |
| interface | use for machines only; when referring to humans use "meet," "discuss," or "interact" |

**more than, over**

| | |
|---|---|
| more than<br>Example: | use with figures<br>The system produces more than 1,000 pages per hour. |
| over<br>Example: | use to refer to spatial relationships<br>The satellite flies directly over New York. |

**principal, principle**

| | |
|---|---|
| principal (noun) | chief of a school, person chiefly liable in a legal proceeding, a sum of money drawing interest |
| principal (adjective)<br>Example: | chief, primary, most fundamental<br>The company's three principal divisions are as follows: |
| principle (noun)<br>Example: | fundamental truth, belief, or law<br>The method involves three guiding principles. |

**prioritization, prioritize** — do not use; use "assigning priority" or "assign priority"

so — use only with "that," as in "so that. . ."

## SAMPLE C: PAGE FORMAT

### Format Guide for Proposal Writers

The formatted file you received contains the following styles. Ultimately, your page should look something like the attached example.

| | |
|---|---|
| Heading1, Heading2, Heading3, Heading4, Heading5 | Section headings to five digits. Heading1 is centered at the top of a new page. Other headings are aligned to the left. Use a tab between the section number and the section name. |
| Theme | The theme statement, which immediately follows the section heading to the 2-digit heading level. |
| Titles | Figure and table titles and action captions. Figure titles belong below the figure. Table titles belong above the table. Use this format. Figure 2-1: Hardware Configuration. This hardware configuration maximizes performance and minimizes cost. |
| Body | Format for the proposal narrative, exclusive of section headings, theme statements, bullets, and figure or table titles. |
| Placehldr | Place holder for a figure or table that will be created in a graphics software program. It drops in a frame. When you've received a graphic tracking number from the artist, type the number into this place holder. |
| Header/Footer | Text formats and lines for headers and footers. These are already in place. Please don't change them. |
| Table | Format for text in tables. Select the entire table before selecting this format. |
| Bullet | Sets the hanging indents for bulleted paragraphs or phrases. Use a space before and after bullets. |

**Header**

Shannon Associates

RFP IRS970005

**Heading**

## SECTION 1: TECHNICAL APPROACH

### 1.1 Developing, Testing, and Maintaining Software

*Senior engineers with a combined 400 years of NASA mission experience have adapted Shannon Associates' methodologies for developing, testing, and maintaining from space-tested systems. The result is software with overall reliability of 5 years mean time between failure, 99.99% availability, and 10-minute repair or replacement.*

**Theme**

NASA programs demand software that is more reliable, maintainable, and available than software developed for nearly any other purpose. Clearly, software that fails on the ground or in the air endangers both lives and mission goals.

Shannon Associates' modular approach to developing, testing, and maintaining software provides procedures to:

**Title**

- Isolate and track the smallest possible units from development through maintenance
- Debug software using a fully computerized model of the spacecraft
- Pinpoint failed modules within five minutes
- Replace failed modules within 10 minutes
- Repair failed modules with 15 minutes

**Bullet**

These features were designed by senior engineers with long experience on the Hubble Space Telescope, Space Station Freedom, and the Space Shuttle orbiter. These engineers were team leaders in developing mission-critical software for launch, orbit, rendezvous, and descent that performed reliably for many years.

As those software systems have been replaced with less cumbersome, modern components, our engineers have adapted the methodologies used with them. Shannon Associates' updated, proven methodologies produce the same reliability with even more availability and maintainability.

**Table**

**Footer**

#### 1.1.1 Approach to Developing Software

*Shannon Associates designs units of software for 10-minute replacement or repair. Systems are never compromised by software failure.*

**Heading 3**

Figure 1.1.1-1 illustrates our software development process.

**Placeholder**

**Figure 1.1.1-1. Shannon Associates' Software Development Process.** We design units for replacement or repair in five minutes.

The features and benefits of our process appear in Table 1.1.1-1.

**Table 1.1.1-1. Features and Benefits of the Development Process.** Our approach is proven to provide fast change-out of mission-critical modules.

| Feature | Benefit |
|---|---|
| Requirements gathering covers mechanical, human, and replacement requirements | Failed units are identified, replaced, or repaired in 10 minutes through human-friendly mechanical systems |
| Units are fully designed for replacement before coding | Units are never broken after coding, preserving the unit integrity and preventing errors |
| Units are coded in parallel | If the government wishes, coding can move faster or slower to meet coordinated schedules |

Use and disclosure of the information on this page is subject to the restrictions on the title page of this proposal.

Page 1

## SAMPLE D: GRAPHIC SUBMITTAL FORM

Author:    Attached a copy of the draft graphic to this form.

Author:    Enter figure/table title:

_____

Author:    Enter proposal format (check one):

_____ single column

_____ double column

Author:    Enter preferred figure/table size (select number from the examples below): _____

Artist:    Assigned a figure tracking number: _____

## SAMPLE E: REVIEW RESPONSE FORM

Volume:

Section:

Is this section complete and compliant? (Yes/No):
For example, is it compliant with Sections C, L, and M? Is it organized so that the most important information stands out and is obvious to the reviewer? Is the section complete? Are the right examples used? The right graphics? Do the graphics support the text and vice versa? Are the theme statements and action captions complete and meaningful?

If not, name at least three things that could be done to make the section complete and compliant:

1.

2.

3.

Other suggestions:

The overall rating for this section is (green, blue, red):

The resources needed to make this section complete and compliant are as follows (name specific people who can provide writing, marketing, technical assistance):

1.

2.

## SAMPLE F: REVIEW INSTRUCTIONS

### Proposal Review Instructions

You have been asked to review the following section or sections of the _____ proposal _____. So that the proposal team receives the "best value" from this review, we ask you to follow these guidelines for your written and spoken remarks.

### General Instructions

1. Read your assigned section and mark your proposal.

2. Meet with any reviewers who are reviewing the same section.

3. Complete the review forms and/or rate the sections.

4. Develop three strategies for improving deficient sections.

5. Convene with the review team.

6. Review your assessment with other reviewers.

7. Prepare slides with other reviewers.

8. Present results to the proposal team.

### Expressing Your Opinions

Provide *constructive* criticism, following these guidelines:

1. Forbidden comments: "This section misses the point entirely"; "They're clearly asking for. . ."; "Just answer the mail."

2. Refrain from sharing negative interpretations, unless they are critical to an argument for or against a particular strategy.

3. In your markup, suggest new wording without saying why.

4. Own your comments by using "I think. . . ."

5. Be specific and thorough. Use sentences rather than phrases.

6. For big problems, coordinate your response with other reviewers and the entire review team.

7. Identify a solution for each problem.

## The Rating Scheme

You will be rating the proposal according to the extent to which it satisfies the following criteria:

- *Compliance:* Is this section compliant with Sections C, L, and M?

- *Organizational Issues:* Is this section organized in such a way that the most important information stands out and is obvious to the reviewer?

- *Content Issues:* Is the section complete? Are the right examples used? The right graphics? Do the graphics support the text and vice versa?

- *Stylistics Issues:* Are the theme statements and action captions complete and meaningful?

Use the following rating scheme to complete the review form (Sample E) according to the your final rating:

- *Green:* This section is ready to go as it stands or with minor revisions.

- *Blue:* This section needs work; provide three or more solid suggestions for improvement.

- *Red:* This section needs a significant overhaul; provide three or more solid suggestions for improvement and identify resources that could be used to make the repairs.

# Index